North American Indian Mythology

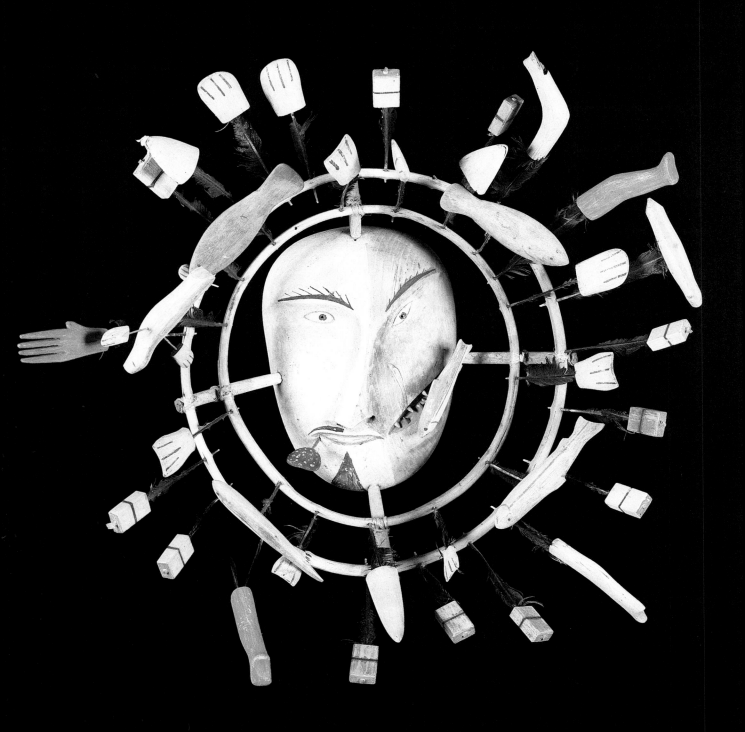

LIBRARY OF THE WORLD'S
MYTHS AND LEGENDS

North American Indian Mythology

Cottie Burland
Revised by Marion Wood

PETER BEDRICK BOOKS
NEW YORK

Half-title page. A wooden construction and mask of the Kwakiutl Indians from Vancouver Island, B.C. It represents a sea-monster, with a separate headpiece of a duck, on top of a human head. It was used in the spring dance ceremonials when its ferocious appearance was intended to drive the salmon towards the shore. Museum of the American Indian, Heye Foundation, New York.

Frontispiece. Aleut mask used by a shaman who has contact with the spirits. The rings represent heaven and earth, and the small wood carvings, attached to birds' quills represent the spiritual helpers. The Aleut groups inhabit the Aleutian Islands, off Alaska. Although linguistically related to the Inuit, their culture was different because the environment was less harsh. Their culture disappeared under the impact of the Russian fur trade. Royal Scottish Museum, Edinburgh.

Published by
Peter Bedrick Books
2112 Broadway
New York, NY 10023

Published by agreement with
The Hamlyn Publishing Group Ltd.
part of Reed International Books.

Library of Congress Cataloging in Publication Data

Burland, C. A. (Cottie Arthur), 1905–
   North American Indian mythology.

   (Library of the world's myths and legends)
   Bibliography: p.
   Includes index.
   1. Indians of North America—Religion and mythology.
I. Title. II. Series.
E98.R3B96   1985   299'.72   85–70555

ISBN 0-87226-248-0 (pbk)

ISBN 0-87226-016-X

Produced by Mandarin Offset
Printed in Hong Kong
10 9 8 7 6 5 4 3
Third printing 1991

Contents

Introduction

The North American continent is an immense, roughly triangular land mass. It extends from the permanent ice-cap of the arctic to the sub-tropical regions of California and Florida. In the west there are great mountain chains running from north to south, spreading out into two main regions with a dry valley between them in the region of Utah. Over on the east coast there are other, much older mountain ranges, the Appalachians, and, in the north, a low rocky plateau of archaean rock known as the Canadian Shield. Between these two major mountainous areas there are wide stretches of alluvial plains, the valley of the Mississippi and Missouri and the prairie region. To the north the plains were scoured out during the last Ice Age and the glacial moraines have produced a region where the low sandy hills have dammed up the waterways to form the Great Lakes system and Hudson Bay. Within this whole vast area there are few natural barriers which would hinder the passage of man.

Archaeologists believe that men first entered America some 25,000 years ago, although there is little evidence of occupation before the ending of the last Ice Age around 12,000 years ago. The route of immigration was from Siberia across the Bering Strait to Alaska. During the last glaciation a fall in the sea level exposed a broad land bridge linking the two continents and thus allowing bands of nomadic hunters to cross over in pursuit of the herds of game animals on which they depended for food. We can assume that these early inhabitants of North America had already developed a form of culture enabling them to survive the severe climatic conditions – warm skin clothing, for example, and some type of habitation. With the melting of the ice cap, a wide ice-free corridor was formed along the eastern fringe of the Rockies towards the Great Plains and through this gap the wandering hunters spread southwards, into regions of more equable climate. Many archaeological sites dated to between 12,000 and 8,000 years ago have produced evidence of their skill in working stone tools and weapons, which are often found in association with the bones of extinct Pleistocene mammals, such as mammoth, bison and camel.

For millions of years the animal population of North America had thrived, and there can be no question that the country was ideal for hunters. Of these very ancient times we have no clear echoes in North American Indian legends. There are one or two tales, collected among the Naskapi of Labrador, which tell of creatures able to push over trees. It is not certain whether these were folk tales of the mammoth, or whether they were ultimately derived from stories told by European visitors. The Norsemen, for instance, for 400 years from the early 11th century, visited the coasts of Newfoundland and Labrador to collect timber for use in the Greenland settlements. It may well be that Indians in contact with these Norse visitors were regaled with stories of strange lands far away,

Opposite. The main tribal areas of North America.

6

North American Indian Culture Areas

Inuit (Eskimo)

Fishermen of the Northwest Coast
Principal tribes *Haida, Kwakiutl, Tlingit, Tsimshian, Nootka*

Hunters of the Northern Forests
Principal tribes *Cree, Ojibwa, Algonquin, Naskapi*

Farmers of the Eastern Woodlands
Principal tribes *Iroquois, Huron, Delaware*

Buffalo Hunters of the Plains
Principal tribes *Sioux (or Dakota), Blackfoot, Arapaho, Cheyenne, Comanche*

Hunters of the Great Desert
Principal tribes *Navajo, Apache, Papago*

Farmers of the Southeastern Woodlands
Principal tribes *Cherokee, Choctwa, Creek, Natchez, Seminole*

Dwellers on the Mesas
Principal tribes *Hopi, Zuni*

Above. 'Bear Bull, a Blackfoot shaman'
Photographed by Edward S. Curtis (1868-
1952). From the 1890s Curtis, a Seattle
photographer, made it his life's work to
compile a comprehensive pictorial record
of the native American peoples, believing
them to be a 'vanishing race'. This
ambitious undertaking, completed after
thirty years of obsessive and painstaking
labour, resulted in *The North American
Indian.* This monumental work comprised
twenty volumes of illustrated text and
twenty portfolios of photographs.

Opposite. An Alaskan 'Eskimo family',
photographed by Curtis.

where creatures like the elephant
were found.

All ancient immigration into the
Americas was by the race which we
know as Amerindian. Human skeletal
remains from early archaeological
sites are extremely rare, but the
evidence does suggest that the ancestors of the North American Indians
were already a mixed race, of Mongoloid affinities, from the time of their
first entry into the North American
continent.

There is no evidence of a planned
migration or invasion at any time.
The likelihood is that, over a period
of thousands of years, people found
their way into the country in family
groups, during hunting expeditions.
Finding the land full of game, with
extra resources of wild berries, edible
tubers and other plants, they settled
down, making their way from place
to place, and leaving no trace for the
archaeologist, beyond the occasional
remains of a camp fire and a few
stone implements scattered throughout the land over which they roamed.
On linguistic grounds we may
suppose that, at some time more
than 1,000 years ago, there was a
movement of tribes along the foothills
of the Rockies and then eastwards
across the Great Plains into the
Atlantic seaboard areas. It was probably part of a great spiralling
migration of tribes which was still in
progress when the European settlements along the east coast first began
to be developed.

There were some hundreds of
distinct linguistic groups in the North
American population and few of
them had anything in the way of a
migration legend. They generally
assumed that man was created first in
the regions that they themselves
inhabited. At the time of the
discovery of North America by Europeans the Indians had no written
records, so it is pointless to hope for
much depth in the time scale of their
legends. Many of the eastern tribes
had mnemonic systems, such as the
famous wampum belts of the
Iroquoian tribes. Among the Ojibwa
there were inscribed birchbark scrolls
which recorded pictorially a sequence

of events in the mythical stories of tribal heroes. But in general stories were passed down to the youngsters by elders of considerable repute. Not everyone could be a custodian of the tribal histories; the job fell only to those either with specially trained memories or with a special aptitude for telling the stories.

There is a wide variation in stories from the different regions because of the great cultural diversity of the North American continent. In the north there were the Eskimo or Inuit, an ice-hunting people who had evolved a remarkable culture which enabled them to survive under extremely harsh conditions. The Caribou Eskimo, inland, followed the migrating caribou. In the northern forest area, north of the Great Lakes, the forest tribes, mostly of Cree origin, were living as a forest-hunting people, their lives dependent on the migration of caribou and the tracking of deer, beaver and smaller animals.

In the Eastern Woodlands, that is to say the northeastern United States and southeastern Canada, many tribes were settled in semi-permanent villages by the time of the first European contact, and already possessed a basic farming culture that was more important than the hunting side of their economy. They had learnt about maize agriculture from tribes to the south of them and had themselves established apple orchards and cared for many other vegetables including pumpkins and beans. Each village might consist of 1,000 or more inhabitants living in bark-covered longhouses. Between one village and another there was easy transport by means of birchbark canoes, which not only carried parties of young men on the warpath, but also served as the vehicles of inter-tribal trade. The

foundation of the League of the Iroquois in the latter part of the 16th century, was made possible by their settled economy. Other tribes, more dependent on hunting, relied on less permanent dwellings called wigwams, which were simple round or rectangular structures of poles covered with bark sheets or rush mats.

Farther to the south, in the warmer areas, such tribes as the Cherokee were living in confederations of villages which might contain as many as 2,000 individuals. Each village was under the authority of a chief, or sometimes of a chieftainess, and most of them were formed into loose confederations for better trading relationships between each other and the tribes around. They were an advanced agricultural people, and their whole ceremonial life was linked to the passage of the seasons and the development of the crops.

The whole of the central plains region south of the Great Lakes was inhabited, before the introduction of the horse in about 1700, by tribes practising a mixed economy. They lived among the small patches of woodland in the river valleys, building earth houses to withstand the winter snows and, to enable them to become more mobile, living in skin tipis during the hunting seasons. Their hunting of the migrating herds

of buffalo brought ample food supplies. As well as using their stone-tipped spears and arrows, they resorted to stratagem, creating pitfalls by planting rows of upright posts that served to divert part of the herd over a cliff, so that the fallen animals could be more easily slaughtered at the base. This was a different life from that of the horsemen who depended almost entirely on buffalo meat in the century before the final destruction of independent Indian life in the late 19th century, and who also used stratagem in hunting. Farming, particularly for the tribes of the eastern Plains, was also important and at least half of the foodstuff of the village in earlier times was produced by women working on their garden plots to grow vegetable food. The legends of the Indians of the Plains reflect the world of the hunter as well as displaying an interest in agricultural matters.

On the Rocky Mountain borders of the Pacific, and on the island chains of Vancouver Island and the Queen Charlotte Islands, there lived highly specialised groups of seafaring tribes. The abundance of fish, seal and sealion enabled them to achieve a high degree of artistic culture and to live in considerable comfort without resorting to agriculture, although some berries, leaves and roots were collected and formed part of their

Above. An Eskimo of Eskimo Point, the Northwest Territories proudly holds his carving. The skill of the Inuit (Eskimos) dates back to the ritual carvings and the decoration of the weapons and utensils of their predecessors – the people of the Dorset and Thule cultures.

In 1959 the Canadian Guild of Crafts set up a cooperative – now run by the Inuit themselves – to market these objects which are a tangible link with their culture.

Left. Present-day Indians carving a totem pole, British Columbia.

Left, below. A Chilkat blanket with a repeated killer whale design. This type of design is known as the 'hocker' motif and its distinctive feature is the figure with limbs outstretched in frog fashion. The joints of limbs were often marked with faces and eyes. The usual colours are black, white, blue and yellow. Made of cedar bark fibres and goat hair, 19th century. Horniman Museum, London.

Opposite, left. Pomo woven basket with human figures. Feathers and shell beads on rim. California. Museum of the American Indian, Heye Foundation.

Opposite right. Petroglyphs showing a buffalo hunt, found along the Saline River valley in Russell County, Kansas. The acquisition of horses made hunting much easier for the Plains tribes.

Above. The Pueblo Indians had the most fully developed mythology of all the North American peoples. They believed in spirits called kachinas, who had specific functions to perform in the agricultural festivals. This Indian painting shows Tawa, the sun kachina. Smithsonian Institution, Washington, D.C. Bureau of American Ethnology.

Opposite. When the Europeans reached North America they found advanced Indian communities living in the southeast. This engraving of the village of Secota, Virginia, summarises Indian life as it appeared to the explorer: the bark-covered wigwams, the cultivated fields, the ceremonial dances, the deer hunt and the sacred fire of carved logs. Drawing by John White, 16th century.

diet. Their beautifully made tools and weapons consisted of adzes, chisels, hammers, daggers, spears and so on. Blades of flaked stone and shell were replaced with metal ones after contact with Europeans. Since wars between villages were common, the stories have a tendency towards the heroic adventure tale, while the shamans, or medicine-men, were interested in stories about the origins of animals, civilisation and life after death.

To the south, in the main Rocky Mountain-Pacific Coast areas of the United States, the country was inhabited by very poor hunting tribes who practised a little agriculture to supplement the vegetable resources available in the form of acorn flour and wild roots and berries. The wildness of the country and the general aridity tended to make conditions so

hard that tribes remained small and poverty-stricken. This was some protection, since their richer eastern neighbours of the Plains felt no advantage, and indeed no honour, in raiding such poor and primitive people.

In the southwestern areas, Utah and Colorado, North American Indian culture reached its highest point. For many centuries there had been agricultural life centring around large mud-built villages along the river valleys in the desert. Some of these Indians, notably the Hohokam people, practised irrigation, digging trenches running from higher to lower levels of the river system so as to fertilise their fields. But when the climate deteriorated in the 12th century, many of the village settlements became untenable and agriculture became concentrated on the fertile parts of the river valleys, while the villages were moved into the wasteland beyond.

However, the droughts had stricken the Plains tribes as well, and they developed the habit of raiding the more settled Indian communities. This was partly guarded against by the removal of the villages into caves and into fortified pueblos, or town settlements, on the tops of isolated mesas. The tribes of Pueblo Indians were of more than one linguistic group, but they had a basic common culture conditioned by the circumstances of their life. They had the most clear-cut mythology of all the North American peoples and the most carefully organised social system, in which religion and social life were carefully planned on the basis that a man growing up in the community would move from one office to another, holding power alternately in civil and religious fields. Thus, the chief, who was really the law-giver and adviser to the community as a whole, reached his political position only after having been thoroughly initiated into the religious and traditional knowledge of his people.

The approach to the mythology of North America is through different levels of culture. It is not a journey

through time. The contemporary state of tribes in the 16th century varied from the very simple life of stone-age hunters, with no agriculture at all, to the organised town settlements of the Pueblo Indians and the Cherokee. In fact, in the lower Mississippi area, tribes such as the Natchez built settlements on mounds and were the only people in the North American continent known to be divided into castes of aristocrats, priests and commoners in a highly organised social system with very advanced social contacts between the towns. Their craftsmanship was also of a high order. Nearly all of this, however, was destroyed in the first century of the European invasions of the continent and little was left to tell us about the way of life of these advanced tribes.

Above. The signing of the Fort Laramie treaty in 1868 in which the Sioux were promised that they could keep the Black Hills. A few years later, when gold was found in the area, the government withdrew the Indians' title to the land.

Above, top. 'Class in American History' from the Hampton Album (1899-1900), in itself a fascinating study of cultures. The Museum of Modern Art, New York. Gift of Kirstein Lincoln.

Opposite, top. 'Ceremonies performed by Saturiona of the Timucua before going on an expedition against the enemy.' From an engraving by De Bry after a drawing by Le Moyne, who visited Florida in 1564–65.

Right. Prisoners at Fort Bowie. The Indians were soon reduced to a state far removed from the earlier – and later – romanticised idea of them.

The Inuit (Eskimo)

The word 'Eskimo' to describe a member of this race of arctic nomads appears to be Algonquin Indian for 'raw-meat eater'. The term was adopted by early French explorers, being first recorded in 1611, and later by the English. Today most Eskimos regard this name as somewhat pejorative and prefer to call themselves 'Inuit', which simply means 'men'.

Inuit folk tales hold the position of myths as there is almost no formalised group of beliefs about a pantheon of gods. The material is limited by the nature of Inuit experience. No Inuit would recount legends of the great forest, or of a life in which people dug the ground in order to make plants grow. The natural environment of the Inuit was very grim, although it had a fantastic beauty of its own.

Life for the Inuit was always precarious. A season of successful hunting meant that there would be comfort and the euphoria of success for everyone. It would bring about periods of jollity and happiness, and of eating and drinking to excess. But it was also a time of preparing stocks of dried meat and fish in readiness for the times when success was not so widespread. Food would be carefully buried against such times and, although it might be in a curious condition when dug up again, being often dry and mouldy and smelling like old cheese, such stores remained edible for a long time. And, of course, while the camps were being re-established in the spring, it was necessary to have immediate resources of nourishing food available until regular hunting could begin again. The presence of such caches of food, sometimes forgotten or lost over many years, led to stories of spirits who revealed special supplies of food to wandering heroes.

The times when the ice froze, or broke up, were periods when the whole way of life of the people would change with the aspect of the natural world, and this was reflected in their stories. The summer hunting of walrus and whale on the open sea inlets provided exciting material for adventure tales. The winter periods of waiting for the caribou to come or for fish and seals at blowholes in the ice gave occasion to many strange stories of ghosts and fantastic creatures who appeared from the darkness.

The world of the Inuit was always filled with mystery. Birds flew to unknown lands uttering cries which were taken as a presage for good or evil. The aurora borealis danced in the sky, and people saw in it images of their own families and friends who had passed out of this world and were now dancing happily around fires in the heavens. They would call out greetings and ask them to send good luck to their descendants upon earth. The sea itself, the great source of life to the Inuit, from which most of their food was derived, was the home of powerful spirits, notably a very ancient fertility mother. The Old Woman who lived under the sea was the nearest thing to a true deity among the Inuit. In various parts of the arctic she was known under different names – Nerivik in Alaska and Arnarquagssag in Greenland, for example. Sedna was the name in use in the central area.

'Eskimo Jackson', a Curtis photograph.

Sedna

The basic legend makes this personage a typical example of the great Earth Mother concept common to all mythologies. A Central Inuit story tells that once there were two giants. Nobody knows how they came into being or who they were. They just existed, living, as the Inuit do, by hunting. They had a child, a girl, who grew up rapidly and showed a terrifying inclination to seize on flesh and eat it whenever she could find it. She was abnormally hungry, even for a giant's child. One night she started to eat the limbs of her parents as they slept. They awoke in horror, seized the frightening child and took her in an umiak (one of the large, skin-covered boats used for transport and whale hunting) far out into the deeper parts of the sea. There they started cutting off her fingers. As the fingers fell into the water they turned into whales, seals and shoals of fish. The giant parents became even more frightened by this so they threw the child into the sea and paddled themselves home as fast as possible. The story recounts that they lived to be very, very old and finally fell asleep and were frozen to death in a way common to many Inuit people. The demon girl, living under the waters, became Sedna, the great mother of all the sea creatures. It was she who caused storms on the sea, and she who governed the migration of her myriads of children – the whales and walruses, the seals and fish of all kinds. The Inuit did not conceive of change, but believed that she was always there and could be approached by shaman in trance.

On occasions when shortage of food threatened, the shaman would go into a trance and his soul would soar over the sea until he came to a great whirlpool. Then he would be drawn down and find himself in a beautiful tent under the sea, furnished with the skins of all manner of sea animals. There, seated on a bench, was the great dark lady herself. She would listen to the requests of her people, sung as a hymn by the soul of the shaman. He would dance and contort himself in front of her to

engage her attention and amuse her, so that she would feel favourably inclined towards his people. Eventually she would give him a message, either threatening that the people would die unless they moved to another place, or promising that food would come abundantly from her inexhaustible stores. The soul of the shaman would then be returned to his body. He would become conscious after the trance and sing a magical song recounting what Sedna had told him, and the people would act in accordance with her wishes.

The shaman

Among all the Inuit a great spiritual power was attached to the shaman or

Above. A carved wooden half-figure wearing a mask. Large Eskimo figures such as this are rare. Point Barrow, Alaska. University of Pennsylvania Museum, Philadelphia.

Top. Carving of an owl *c.* 1968 by Qirluag of Repulse Bay, Northwest Territories. National Museum of Man, Ottawa.

Right. On the frozen Bering Sea near Nome, Alaska.

angakok. Usually the candidate for these powers was inspired to wander in a deserted area when he reached the age of puberty. After a few days hunger and anxiety dissociated him from his environment, and then the tornaq, or spirit, appeared to him, usually in some near-human form. There was a dialogue between them. The frightened aspirant was promised strength and visions. He returned to his family and for a time lived a normal life, but spells of inspiration came, and eventually he sought to be accepted as an assistant to an experienced magician, from whom he could receive training in shamanistic skills, such as curing illness, controlling the weather and foretelling the future.

The only kind of religious gathering among the Inuit was the impromptu attendance at seances organised, or rather inspired, through the shaman. If he felt himself being overcome by the spirits of nature or the souls of the dead, the shaman would retire to his tent and sit swaying regularly, holding his tambourine-like drum high above his head and beating it with a steady rhythm. People would come together, to sit quietly and watch him falling into a trance. In this state there was always a display of shouting and struggles which looked like a fit. He would scream in strange languages and suffer sickness and nausea. Every now and then his words would make

sense to his audience, for some of them knew the ancient dialects commonly used by magicians. As his words came struggling out, they would strive to hear them.

The prophecies usually referred to minor domestic matters, but sometimes they assumed group importance when they pronounced words from the spirits telling of the coming of shoals of fish, or of movements of seal or caribou. There is no careful record which compares prophecies with actually observed phenomena, but there is every reason to think that a skilled shaman was acutely aware of the state of the weather, and the activities of local animals, which would give him clues. He would

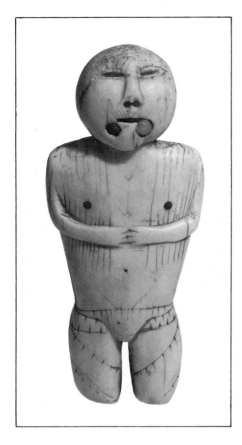

Above. The religious life of the Inuit centred around the seances at which the shaman communicated with the spirit world. This small ivory doll was used as a charm in the ceremonies. The two circular inserts on the face are trade beads and represent the labrets, or lip-plugs, customarily worn by the northern tribes. Banks Island, 1800–1880. Museum of the American Indian, Heye Foundation, New York.

Above, top. Part of a walrus-ivory bow drill engraved with figures of caribou turning into people, and on the left a water-monster emerging from a shaman's hut. The Inuit believed that all animals had spirits which inhabited the animal's body. Museum of Mankind, London.

probably not be able to express these delicate impressions in ordinary, everyday talk, but, when in a trance, this inner knowledge of the situation was projected and appeared in the strange sing-song recital.

Thus, through the ecstatic trance and prophetic powers of their shaman, the Inuit were always in contact with the spirit world of their mythology. There can be little doubt that the shaman usually experienced the visions he described. He was a natural shaman first before he learned the little arts of deception which belong to his professional calling. The visions were of the nature of highly dramatised archetypal dreams and, because the shaman was so steeped in tribal traditions, the setting for the vision was already prepared for him. It was a translation of local Inuit life on to a larger scale or into a different place. For example, the house of the moon man was thought of as a fine igloo up in the sky along the road of the moon. The dead lived in an underworld that was not very happy – rather like this world, only darker – and too often they were hungry because their descendants on earth failed to give them little offerings from their good hunting. It was all very matter of fact and it was felt to be quite practical that the ancestors should inspire the hunter and receive a share of the catch. Life was like that, and for the Inuit seemed likely to go on in the same way for ever.

The spirit world

Because the Inuit was dependent upon the natural world, he therefore felt a relationship between his own inner personality and that of every-thing around him. Bears were not merely soulless animals, but creatures with a spirit of their own, which could be charmed to bring them to the traps and pits of the hunter, but only when this was necessary. Fish were not just animals which swam in

the sea, but creatures provided by the Old Woman who lived under the sea (Sedna). Spirits of all kinds daily watched over the people.

There are a number of Inuit stories which deal with the stars and with the sun and moon. The sun and moon were usually regarded as sister and brother, engaged in a race in which the moon, at first close to his sister the sun, gradually slips behind her until she overtakes him at the end of his course. This is a perfectly natural and observable phenomenon and has given rise to the same story in almost the whole range of humanity. Move-ments of the planets were observed to be irregular, so they were not very important to the seasonal calendar. Astronomy, however, was most important for a hunting people like the Inuit, as a guide to the time of year. The position of the stars at the time of the migration of the caribou, or the appearance of the fish shoals, was very important for the hunter; the whole community needed to know what the position of the stars was just before the freeze up of the long winter nights, and just before the break up of the ice in the spring.

The people in the sky

The following account of the stars was given by Inuit from Smith Sound in northwest Greenland. These people lived so far north that they were able to see the Great Bear to the south of the zenith.

To them, as to all Inuit, the sun is a beautiful girl who carries her torch through the sky as she is chased by her brother the moon, whose name is Aningan. The moon man has a house in which he rests with his demon cousin Irdlirvirisissong, who is a kind of female clown who sometimes comes out into the sky and dances to make people laugh. But if anyone, such as a visiting shaman, is nearby, they had best look sideways, for if they laugh she (the clown) will dry

Above. Man-shaman carved from walrus ivory. The figure is probably a shaman because he is clutching his stomach in a typical shamanistic gesture.

Left. A wooden dance mask used in various feast ceremonies. It was too delicate to be worn and was just held up in front of the face. It represents Negafok the cold-weather spirit – one of the hundreds of Inuit spirits. He looks sad because spring is coming and he must leave the people. Kuskokwim River, Alaska. Museum of the American Indian, Heye Foundation, New York.

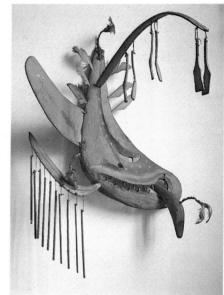

Above. Canadian Inuit family drying fish. Many skills have been lost, but some Inuit are re-discovering the old ways.

Above, right. Kuskokwim Inuit mask. A powerful evocation of the movement of whales through the ocean is achieved by the sweeping plastic form and airy decoration of this mask. It represents a 'spirit-helper' conducting a school of great white whales to the hunters, and was worn by the shaman in the ceremony. Painted wood and feathers, late 19th century. André Breton Collection, Paris.

Right. Inuit inua mask, south-east Alaska. The soul of the salmon is represented on the front of the mask. By wearing such masks in dances and ceremonies, the hunters believed they could increase their magical control over animals' souls and so over their real bodies. The seven pendants are stylised reductions from the fish-shape, and re-inforced the power of the mask magic. Probably 19th century. Painted wood and feathers. André Breton Collection, Paris.

Opposite. An Inuit woman in furs with her baby on her back. A 16th-century watercolour by John White. Museum of Mankind, London.

them up and devour their intestines.

The moon is a great hunter who is always in front of his igloo. His sledge stands piled high with seal skins. He has a sledge team of spotted dogs which sometimes leave the sky and shoot down to earth like shooting stars. The mother of the sun is the planet Jupiter, and she is dangerous to magicians. They have to be wary lest she should eat their livers.

Some of the main constellations of stars also have myths attached to them, connected with their forms. There was once a bear who was chased by a fine pack of dogs. They all ran so hard that they left the earth and came up into the sky where they form the Pleiades – or, to the Inuit, Nanook the bear and the hunting dogs. Over the heads of the Smith Sound Inuit, a giant caribou looks down – he is the constellation Ursa Major. Opposite him, across the sky, are the stones which support a lamp – this is Cassiopeia. Between the two, on the edge of the sky, are three steps cut in a snow bank linking heaven and earth – these are the constellation Orion. Sometimes on a dark night the ancestors dance and light fires – this is the joyful bridge of the aurora, perhaps related to the Gullabrig, the sky bridge in Norse folk lore.

Ancestral spirits

Although the Inuit had no conception of a supreme spirit, some tribes believed that there was one ancestral spirit who came to each family to direct its welfare. But in many regions it was felt that there was an overlord of all the ancestral spirits, very much in the way that European peasants believed in a king of the fairies. This overlord could be approached by shamans and begged to give information, but more reliance was placed on the information given in dreams by the family's ancestors, and on the conjectures of hunters who believed that they had been blessed by the spirits so that they could sometimes understand the speech of birds and animals. The prophecies of the hunters, of course, were again a way of manifesting the information that

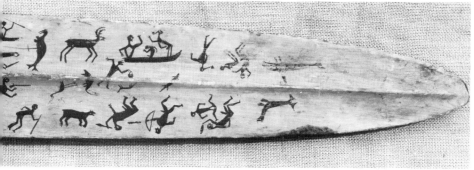

Above. A small wooden figure of an evil spirit, from Greenland. The harsh conditions of Eskimo life gave rise to myths about malignant beings who had to be placated with offerings. Nationalmuseet, Copenhagen.

Opposite, top. Ivory pendant in the form of a two-headed sea-monster with a shaman. It illustrates two allied Inuit beliefs: that the monster can swallow a man's soul and eject it again, and that the shaman has the power to visit the inner world and return at will. Museum of Mankind, London.

Left. A paddle with a painted scene showing hunters, animals and spirits. Hunters sometimes believed that they had been blessed by the spirits and could understand the speech of animals and birds. Museum of Mankind, London.

they had accumulated by observing the natural world around them.

Many of the myths of the Inuit give us a valuable picture of life as it was lived by these people. The stories take one into the ice-hunters' igloos or to the caribou hunters' skin tents. We find all their curious customs reflected. Perhaps surprisingly, we find that, in spite of the harsh and cruel environment, the Inuit were an extremely sensitive people. It was sometimes necessary for them to abandon a child, or to allow their old parents to freeze to death. It was an absolute necessity from time to time, when living as a member of a small band searching for enough to eat, that, when things were really bad, the weaker members should be sacrificed for the welfare of the whole. Nevertheless, every story in which events of this kind happen refers to the sorrow of the people, to their unhappiness at losing those who were dear to them. The pain which they felt at this sacrifice has led to a number of stories of a romantic cast, in which the old people remain under the ground and find means of attracting their descendants to give them useful information, or in which the abandoned child, particularly the abandoned girl, finds a new life of her own, and comes to wonderful land where she marries a fairy prince, finally returning home, rich in furs and ivory, to her aged parents.

Inuit myths show a human community fighting its environment, making use of everything possible to sustain life and usually winning through the struggle. If unsuccessful, whole tribes simply vanished.

The Fishermen of the Northwest Coast

The Indians who lived along the west coast of North America, from southern Alaska through British Columbia and south as far as northern California, developed an intricate tribal organisation and a highly specialised technology, which allowed them to exploit to the full their natural surroundings. Physically, they were of typical North American Indian stock, with a generally Mongoloid appearance, the characteristic straight black or dark brown hair and reddish-brown skin colour which varied considerably within any one tribe.

The environment of the North Pacific Coast is rich in natural resources. The coast is rocky, with many deep, fiord-like indentations, and scattered offshore islands. The structure was determined geologically by the incursion of the sea into valleys of the rocky mountains as they slowly sank lower in the ocean. Many of the valleys were steep-sided and highly glaciated. The whole country was heavily wooded, the chief timber trees being cedar and Douglas fir.

The Indians themselves were conditioned, probably over thousands of years, to a life of fishing and hunting. The ocean was prolific. There were immense numbers of fish, herds of seal and great numbers of seabirds. The Indians fished the sea from magnificent watercraft. Dug-out canoes, sometimes forty or fifty feet (twelve to fifteen metres) in length, each capable of holding crews of thirty or forty men, were a common means of transport. Inland, they were particularly fortunate in the immense shoals of salmon which every year ascended and descended the rivers and were trapped in their thousands.

Not only was the fish eaten fresh, it was also dried and great quantities of salmon oil were extracted during the drying process, to be stored in wooden bowls. Some of these bowls, even after nearly 200 years of storage in museums, still ooze salmon oil.

In the woods of the mainland animal food was available. In some regions caribou and deer were plentiful; in all areas there were bears and many smaller edible mammals. Vegetable products consisted mainly of wild seeds and berries and there were a number of edible roots which could be pounded up and made into

something resembling a hard, unleavened bread. Edible fungi and mosses were also sought out. Agriculture was not practised.

The Northwest Coast Indians were, in theory at least, a pre-agricultural stone-age population when the first European sailors visited their coasts in the 18th century. However, the degree of comfort in their lives was quite remarkable when compared with that of other Indian tribes.

Village life

The population was large. Inhabitants of a village might vary in number from 100 to 200 up to as many as 1,000 individuals. Villages were normally built near the mouths of the rapidly flowing mountain rivers. Such a site was a convenient place for beaching the canoes and a sheltered background was important because it helped to deter raids by other tribes. Houses differed from tribe to tribe, but all were square or rectangular structures of heavy wooden posts and beams with cedar planking for walls and roofs. A doorway, either round or oval, was placed in the gable-end facing the shore.

The Indians of the Northwest Coast were superbly conditioned to exploit the immense resources available to them. The fish, seals and seabirds of the coast and ocean were but one of these resources, which enabled them to develop an intricate and highly creative tribal organisation. They fished the ocean with magnificent dug-out canoes, which may have been up to fifty feet (fifteen metres) long.

Above. Head of a totem figure, seven feet tall (two metres), carved by the Kwakiutl Indians, Queen Charlotte Islands, B.C. Taylor Museum Colorado Springs Fine Arts Center.

Opposite. Carved wooden crouching figure of a man, wearing a bear's-head hat. This is a copy of a grave marker from Cat Island. This replica totem is at Totem Bight, near Ketchikan, Alaska.

Technology

The basic structure of life depended largely upon the use of tools capable of cutting down big trees and shaping them into the magnificent houses and canoes which were the means of tribal life. The normal stone-age hunter, with his chipped stone arrow heads and flaked knives, such as were used by the Inuit, could not deal with forest country. The Northwest Coast Indians, however, developed efficient axes and adzes made out of hard polished stone. Sometimes their tools had very handsome sculptural decoration on them. The blades were lashed to wooden handles by hide thongs and were quite as efficient as the white man's steel, albeit slower. Their woodworking showed great craftsmanship and a wide range of items were made out of wood — boxes, dishes, clubs, masks, rattles and so on. Ornamentation was done by painting and by carving in relief.

There is also a wide range of stone sculpture known from this area although it is all on a small scale. It was produced by chipping and beating at the stone with other pieces of rock, and then polishing and grinding the shapes so obtained with sand and wood until a smoothly contoured surface was achieved.

There was little knowledge of metal before the time of the white man, although nodules of natural copper were beaten out to make ceremonial objects, such as the shield-shaped plates called coppers, which had a high prestige value. Examples of these are to be found in museums today, although almost all of these have been made from copper sheeting taken from the bottom of wrecked or abandoned ships.

Textile fibres were produced by beating out cedar-bark and by spinning mountain-goat wool. Among the Salish, dog hair was also used, although rather more rarely. These fibres were hung on an upright wooden framework and then twined by the weaver's fingers, working from top to bottom. This technique of finger twining was used to make large knee-length cloaks which were worn tied over the chest and little wrap-around aprons which reached from the hip to just above the knee. Men generally went naked in the warmer weather, but also wore tunics of woven plant fibre, while women wore fringed fibre skirts. Both sexes wore beautifully woven basketry hats, often painted with elaborate designs. One style, worn by people of high rank, was topped with four small cylindrical elements, all woven in one piece.

The totem

The organisation of fishing expeditions, hunting and war parties demanded that there should be system of government that was to some extent permanent. This took a form similar, in some ways, to the feudal system in Europe. The important families of the tribe were divided into totemic groups, not unlike the clans of Scotland in their social organisation. They dedicated themselves to the honour of the family totem, almost like a clan ancestor. Thus, there were the Bear People, the Killer Whale People, the Cannibal Spirit People, Salmon People, Beaver People and so on. This did not mean that they believed themselves to be descended from those particular animals or spirits, or even to have had a common ancestry, in the way understood by Australian aborigines. Rather, they adopted these names to commemorate the roles which these beings had played in the tribal myths, often in assisting legendary ancestors of the tribe. The totem, in fact, had much in the nature of a family crest. The people of the bear totem, for example, would have bear symbols on their clothing, and their houses would be built with finely carved totem poles exhibiting representations of the bear.

These totem poles, for which the Northwest Coast region is famous, had various functions. As well as forming the structural members of a house, they could be erected to commemorate a person or an event, or to symbolise a special privilege. In the 19th century, when the Indians obtained fine steel tools in trade with the white man, they were able to

develop larger and more elaborately carved totem poles.

The carving of the totem on the pole also had an important bearing on social custom. If a stranger from another village came visiting in time of peace, the first thing he did was to look at the totem poles to see which house belonged to members of his own totemic group. He could then go there expecting to find protection, food and shelter. He was accepted as a kinsman, to be supported against other families in the village, and against any raiding by other tribal groups while he stayed there. This was a very important point, because it allowed the spread of tradition from one group to another. It also preserved ancient customs by making sure that, in every region within visiting distance of others, the old stories were repeated, and the old beliefs about the spirits, the origins of fire and other myths, were basically the same.

It is natural that the folk tales of the Northwest Coast Indians should be concerned with hunting adventures, both on land and sea, with the relationship between family and totemic groups, and, of course, with the various war cults. War itself was a very common activity during the seasons when hunting was not necessary. The Indians had a tremendous sense of the importance of winning military victories over their neighbours, and prestige raids, both for killing rival tribesmen and for kidnapping slaves, were commonplace events. These raids produced stories of heroic bravery and sometimes strange cruelties. Any stratagem was considered fit for use against an enemy, so some of the tales tell of the curious tricks by which groups of people were trapped and killed or enslaved. Slavery was a misfortune and the slave, although normally treated kindly, as a rather low-grade human being, was the chattel of his or her owner. When the great chiefs held a potlatch festival, during which they gave presents to all the members of a visiting group, they sometimes demonstrated their contempt for property by clubbing slaves to death.

The potlatch festival

The potlatch festival was a means of giving away wealth, or destroying it, to gain social prestige, and also of exchanging useful goods. The group which received the gifts was bound in honour to hold a potlatch festival themselves later, in which they gave back goods exceeding in value those that they had received. Thus, there was a constant transfer of wealth in the form of carved wooden chests, blankets, personal ornaments, tools and in fact all the manufactured goods of the people. It was socially important to make things for use as gifts in these ceremonies as well as for personal everyday use. But there was very little real trade in the normal sense of the word; occasionally blankets or beautiful small carvings were exchanged for food or other objects of value. Normally each village community subsisted on the food gathering and craftwork of its own members without needing to trade with any outside peoples at all.

Ceremonial life

The ceremonial life was richest in the dark months of winter, when the long nights were enlivened by dramatic performances by societies who enacted totemic legends, and by the retelling of myths by the elders, who thereby preserved the tribal lore. Children, although at first frightened by the strange animal masks and paint of the actors in these dramatic recitals, gradually came to learn the

Above. The interior of a house in Nootka Sound, Vancouver Island. At the back are two posts, carved with the totem emblems of the family. Fish hang from racks near the floor to dry in the smoke from the fire. A woman on the left wears the basketwork hats typical of this region. From a drawing by John Webber, 1778.

Opposite. A carved wooden headdress known as 'The Mystery of the Sea'. These headdresses are worn by men enacting scenes from the myths, and the rich decoration and ermine skins reflect the ostentatious nature of the Northwest Coast Indians. University Museum, Philadelphia, Pennsylvania.

stories, and to visualise them within the limits of the tribal art style.

There is not sufficient archaeological evidence to show how long the Northwest Coast artistic styles of representing the legendary creatures of the stories had existed. But this style must have persisted for many centuries, possibly for thousands of years, before the white man came. Many of the objects of daily life were history books in themselves: chiefs had wooden war helmets that had been worn in famous battles of the past, and there were ancient war canoes and sometimes ruined house sites which were associated with stories. Historical and religious legends were closely linked.

Principal gods

The mythology was based on the world of nature, conceived as the abode of spirit powers as well as of men. Animals could be heroes as well as humans, but with the difference that in the heroic tales the totems act like humans but can still change into animal form at will. The organisation of the universe is not clearly described and although a number of the events recounted in the stories concern different powers of nature, they are not related to each other in any system. There was probably some general consensus of opinion that there might be some power, the Chief of the Sky People, who was more powerful than the ordinary spirits, and some idea of inescapable fate, but nothing is clearly formulated. There was the customary Old Woman who lived under the sea, who seems to form a myth in most parts of the world, and is, in fact, a psychological phenomenon. From this general view of the way of life of the Indians we can turn to a study of their stories.

The mythology of the Indians of the Northwest Coast is slightly more advanced than that of the Eskimo, but we find no clear traces of deities, apart from a Sky Being, Sun, Moon and the Trickster-Creator known as the Raven.

Many of the characters in the stories are totem creatures not entirely animal and not entirely human. They are in many ways archetypal forms, but are projected in a special way so that they are not immediately recognisable as mythological deities. The concept of a single godhead is foreign to any primitive culture, and we must expect the stories to display much of the nature of what we would consider folk lore. The individual spirits were seen in visions by the shamans but they were never formally worshipped. There were neither regular ceremonies, nor temples, in the whole of the region;

Right. Masked dancers representing Kotsuis and Hokhokw, mythical bird monsters who appeared in the Hamatsa dance, one of the most important of the Kwakiutl winter ceremonial sequence. Their great snapping beaks are controlled by the dancers by moving strings. Photographed by E. S. Curtis.

Opposite, right. Haida village at Skidegate Inlet, Queen Charlotte Islands, in the latter part of the 19th century. American Museum of Natural History, New York.

Opposite, left. Swaixwe mask with three hooded water birds, which represents a guardian spirit. It is derived from the myth of a boy who plunged into a lake and came to rest on the roof of the house of a supernatural being. He received power from the creature and returned to the world with this mask. Salish, Vancouver Island, 1890–1900. Museum of the American Indian, Heye Foundation, New York.

---

civilisation had not yet taken the vital step of organising the myths into a truly religious tradition.

The Lord of the Sky

The Lord of the Sky is referred to in some of the tales as an old chief. Once the sky was much nearer to the earth than it is now, and this old chief was sometimes annoyed by the constant shouting of children, the beating of drums, and the hullabaloo of war parties. Unable to rest, he would cause the mountains to move or induce earthquakes, so as to destroy the offending tribe or give it a fright.

These characteristics are not unreasonable if one is postulating a sky god. However, it is possible that these legends are derived ultimately from the talk of European visitors. There is something unnatural in this idea of the elderly chief living in his house above the skies. Much more

natural myths are those of Raven and the Old Woman who had the Sun in her house, or of the wondrous land under the sea where the killer whales and sea birds had their ceremonial homes. These are more authentic Indian beliefs.

Semi-divine spirits

The spirits of the dead were thought of as going into an underworld where they could occasionally be reached by their descendants. It was clear to the Indian story tellers at the winter ceremonies that one might go to the land of the dead and find one's relatives. But one could never expect to return if food was accepted in this other land. This is a strikingly international conception of the dangers of visiting the other world and recalls the Greek myth of Persephone who ate part of a pomegranate while she was in the underworld and had to spend part of her life there ever after.

Some of the legends are very beautiful, and we find that the wondrous, semi-divine creatures – the great Thunderbird, the sea-dragons, the men who work marvels – are part human, part animal, and part spirit. The mythological world of the Northwest Coast was the world of the hunter where anything might happen and where spiritual forces were always active. These things are not formalised, except in so far as a traditional folk tale about a strange

event was passed on from generation to generation. In early times the story-teller was under the strict censorship of the audience, most of whom had heard the tale every year since they were children. They protested at any variation, but alterations were made in more recent years. The myths were often recited during the winter months, when actors wearing masks and robes would impersonate the characters described.

The powers of nature were personified to some degree and as such they took revenge when creatures of the natural world were deliberately injured. It was one thing to catch salmon for food; the salmon spirits and river spirits were not worried by this, it was the reason why salmon existed. If people caught more than they needed, however, and then threw the fish away, or carelessly tortured the salmon when they were caught, then retribution from the spirit world could be expected. This often occurred in the form of a volcanic eruption.

The Wolf Clan and the salmon

A story from the Nass River illustrates this. It tells how, in a canyon near the head of the river, there was a wonderful place that the tribespeople could always visit to find salmon and wild berries. The villagers who lived nearby were wealthy enough to trade with others and much respected. As

33

Above. Kwakiutl dance mask. A four-headed mask for use in the Hamatsa (Cannibal) Society dances. Made of cedar bark, commercial paint and cord. The Denver Art Museum, Colorado.

Opposite. Kwakiutl potlatch figure. The potlatch festivals provided an opportunity for the Northwest Coast tribes to display their wealth and grandeur by giving away property. This figure, holding a beaten copper shield, was a sign of its owner's affluence. Taylor Museum, Colorado Springs Fine Arts Center.

time went on, the younger people forgot the old traditions; sometimes they killed small animals and left the carcasses for the crows and eagles to eat. Their elders warned them that the Chief in the Sky would be angered by such foolish behaviour, but nobody heeded them. In one case, when the salmon season was at its height and the fish were swimming up river in their myriads, some of the young men of the Wolf Clan thought it amusing to catch salmon, make slits in the fish's backs, put in pieces of burning pitch pine, and put them back in the water so that they swam about like living torches in the river. It was spectacular and exciting, and they did not think about the cruelty to the salmon, or the waste of a good food fish. The elders as usual protested and as usual the young people took no notice. At the end of the salmon running season the tribe made ready for the winter ceremonies. But as they prepared they heard a strange noise in the distance, something like the beating of a medicine-drum, and grew worried. As there was nothing very threatening about it, the young people began to say, 'Aha, the ghosts wake up, they are going to have a feast too.' The old people guessed that the young men's thoughtlessness in ill-treating the salmon had brought trouble on the tribe. After a while the noises died

down, but within a week or two the beating of drums became louder and louder. Even the young warriors became very careful about what they did, because they were frightened. The old people noted the young men's fear, and said it would be their fault if the tribe perished. Eventually a noise like thunder was heard, the mountains broke open, and fire gushed forth until it seemed that all the rivers were afire. The people tried to escape, but as the fire came down the river, the forest caught fire and only a few of them got away. The cause of the conflagration was said by the shamans to be entirely due to the anger of the spirit world at the torture of the salmon. Thus the powers of nature insisted on a proper regard for all their creatures.

Bear Mother

Another group of stories from the Northwest Coast which has become famous concerns the Bear Mother. The stories can be paralleled with much European folk lore. The theme is that of the young woman who wanders away from her own country and goes into an animal's den, under the impression that she is entering a human household. She loses her sense of time and after what she considers to be a short period is rescued by her relatives. But she has in fact been away long enough to become the mother of animal cubs. The European stories are concerned with the world of the fairies, where Thomas the Rhymer, or some other hero, goes to the underground house of the Fairy Queen and is lost there, without knowledge of time, for a long period.

In the Haida story of Bear Mother, there is an interesting picture of everyday life linked with the mythical world of the Bear Spirits.

The princess Rhpisunt, daughter of the chief of the Wolf Clan, was gathering berries on the mountains with two other young women. As Rhpisunt was walking up into the hills she stepped on a bear's excrement and her foot was smeared. This made her very angry; she said 'This bear was a dirty beast and heedless of where I, a lady, stepped, as if it were somebody important.' She kept grumbling about this all day; whenever she saw one of her friends she would shout out angry remarks about the bears. As the day went on she wandered from the others, farther into the forest. At last she had filled her basket, and turned to go back to their canoe. She had not gone very far when the strap of her basket snapped. All the berries spilled on the ground. She scraped them up and started on her way again. When she called out to her companions there was no answer. Again she felt the straps slipping, so she sat down for a while and tightened them.

Soon she met two young men. One of them spoke to her. 'Beautiful lady, we were sent to bring help. Let us take your pack and lead you.' She didn't recognise them, but she thought they were very handsome, especially the young man who was the leader. Rhpisunt had no care that the trail did not lead down to the canoe but away into the mountain. It was a very good trail, and she went along laughing and chattering all the time. Soon they came to a village with a very large house in the centre. The leader took the princess to the house saying, 'Stay here till I see my father.' He went in and she heard a loud voice coming from inside. 'Did you find what you were seeking?' 'Yes, she

stands outside.' 'Bring her in, that I may see my new daughter-in-law.' Then the young man came out, calling, 'Follow me, my father would see you.' She followed him and saw a huge man sitting at the back of the house. Beside him sat a woman with her eyes closed. Inside bearskin coats were hanging everywhere. Old slaves went around as if near death, sleepy and quiet. The great chief called out, 'Bring the girl here, she must sit near me, and beside you. Spread mats that she who visits me may sit down.' The slaves laid down mats at the feet of their master, and here Rhpisunt and the beautiful young man sat down. While the chief was speaking to his servants the princess felt somebody pinch her, 'Have you any wool or fat? I am Mouse Woman. If you have any wool or fat, I can help you.' The princess took off her woollen earrings and some decorations from her hair and gave them to Mouse Woman. After the little old woman received these ornaments, she disappeared. She soon came back and said, 'The Bear People have taken you. They were offended that you insulted the bears when you stepped on their mess today, and that is why Bear Chief was angry. Now do you have any fat? If you have any to give me I'll protect you. The chief's anger is still great.' The princess had some mountain goat fat which she used to rub on her face to keep her skin smooth. She gave this to the little woman who went away again. She returned. 'When you go outside to relieve yourself, dig a hole to hide your excrement. As soon as you've finished cover it up. Then take a piece of your copper bracelet and put it on top as if that were your excrement; take no notice of anyone watching you, but do this every time. The Prince of the Bears will make you his wife. Be careful. You will always be watched. All these old slaves have been lured away by the Bear People because like you they made fun of the bears. Some of them mutilated the bears that they killed, and many have perished for breaking the taboo of the Bear People.'

The chief sent messengers to call friends to a party to welcome the new

Above. When the myths were recounted to the tribe, masked actors impersonated the main characters. This is a Tsonoqua mask, made of wood with fur eyebrows, and representing a female ogre who devours children. Her presence is announced by a whistling in the forest. Museum of Mankind, London.

Opposite, top. Shaman wearing a fur cloak curing a sick child at Kitwanga, British Columbia, 1910.

Opposite, bottom. (*Left*) Shaman's crown, made of ornamented wood with the points of the crown carved in immitation of mountain-goat horns. (*Middle*) Shaman's wooden rattle painted to represent a death-head. (*Right*) Shaman's wand made of bone carved to represent a raven and (near handle) an eagle's head. This was used for fighting hostile spirits and as a charm to detect witches. Staatliches Museum für Völkerkunde, Dresden.

princess. Before long Rhpisunt went outside to relieve herself and dug a hole as usual behind the bushes. When she had covered it all up, she laid on the earth a piece of copper that she broke off one of her bracelets. Then she sat down and watched. The bears, who had been spying on her, rushed to the place where she had sat and found a piece of copper. They were surprised. 'Look, she's right when she says that our excrement's unpleasant. She leaves real copper behind her.'

They took the copper to the chief. Soon the guests began to arrive. When most of them were there, the chief spoke, and his wife at last woke up and noticed that among the company were many real human beings. She was a terrible creature herself. Her breasts were human heads which were alive and moving about, and bright rays of light shone from her eyes in the underworld house. Bear Chief spoke to his guests

and said, 'This is my daughter-in-law. Whenever you see her in danger, you will protect her. Her children will be the grandchildren of the Bear People.' Then great bowls of mountain goat fat were brought in. These had been made by magic from the cosmetic fat that Rhpisunt had given to the little Mouse Woman.

From now on she was married to the bear. She found that the Bear People never used dry wood for their fires; only water-soaked wood from the bottom of rivers would burn in this underworld. Whenever any of the Bear People went out, they always took with them their bear coats. Once outside they put them on and behaved as animals. Sometimes bears would go out and never return, and then someone would announce that 'Our brother's lip-plug has fallen out.' Lip-plugs, or labrets, were valued highly on the Northwest Coast and these words meant that they had lost their most precious possession, their life. When the time came to move to the winter village, where the houses were warmer, Rhpisunt knew that she was pregnant. She discovered that the new village was hidden among the trees, almost in sight of her own old earthly home. They moved to the houses, and she found that her husband had made a new home in a cave high in a cliff.

At home in the village of Niskae, people had missed Rhpisunt long ago. The chief had sent search parties out. They had followed her trail and found the spot where she had dropped her fruit basket. Then they came to a place where, alongside her footprints, there were great bear's footprints on either side of her. They felt certain she had been killed by the bears. They hunted all over the country, hoping to find her body, because bears never eat human beings; but the old medicine man stated that she was not dead, that she would return, and that she was now not far away. All the hunters went into the hills; they killed many bears but found no sign of the princess. The Bear People were very unhappy that so many of their number had been killed, and the Bear Prince told his wife that they would go to a safe

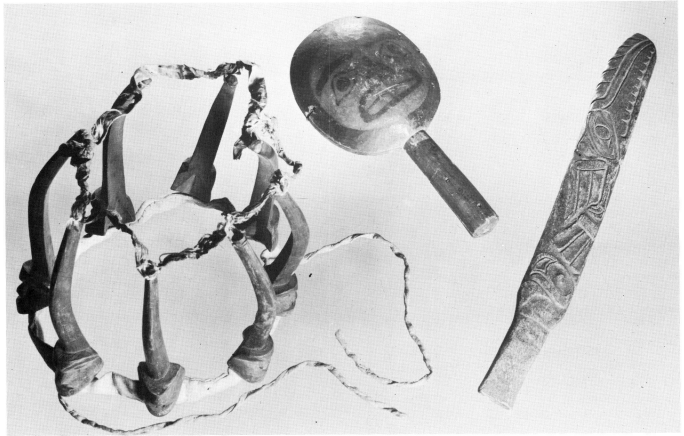

refuge, not far away from her father's village, where she could have her babies in peace. They climbed up into the mountain by a very narrow and dangerous path, but they were safely away from any hunters. Before long the princess gave birth to twin cubs, who grew very fast and were very lively and beautiful.

Among the people from Niskae were the three brothers of Rhpisunt, who all went out seeking her. Her youngest brother and his dog Maesk decided that they would not give up the search as quickly as the other hunters. They roamed far and wide and found nothing. Then they thought of the places where it seemed impossible to go. They arrived at the foot of the cliff, underneath the cave where Bear Mother Rhpisunt and her husband were living. The dog began to howl and her younger brother realised that this meant that she was somewhere very near and that he would have to climb the steep cliff. He slipped back quietly to the village and at every spare moment he practised climbing steep, rocky slopes. The Bear Prince watched from the cave. Every time the hunters came near, he took his family safe into the depths of the cave and said magic words so that the hunters soon became tired and went away. But one day he was very quiet and unhappy. He told his wife that the dog Maesk and his young brother-in-law would

find him and would kill him. Bear Mother was sad, but realised that she must watch for her brother.

One day she saw him on the trail underneath the mouth of the cave and dropped a ball of snow down the side of the mountain. It fell near his feet. When he picked it up, he could see her handprint on it. He held it to his dog's nose and the dog recognised his mistress's scent and began to howl. The younger brother looked up and saw something move across the mouth of the cavern. The hunter and his dog came steadily up the cliff, moving from one tiny foothold to another. The Bear Prince knew that his end was near. He said, 'Let me go to my den, I shall be quite helpless; do not let them mutilate my carcass. When they have skinned me, tell them to burn my bones, and then I may go on to help our children. As soon as I am dead they will turn into humans and become skilful hunters.'

He then prepared to meet his fate. The young hunter came up and did as the bear had prophesied, smoked him out and then speared him. Bear Prince then sang the magical song that he wished the princess and her brother to learn. They promised him they would give the bearskin to his father-in-law, so that he should always have good fortune and the children should be happy in a rich household. All was done as he commanded. The two little bear cubs

trotted along with their mother and uncle and came to the village of their grandfather. As they entered the door of the chief's house, they took off their bearskin coats and became two handsome little boys. Later on, when the magic song and the bear coat had made the chief very wealthy, and the little boys had grown up to be great hunters, their grandfather made a high pole for them to climb up. From the top of the pole they would look out and see smoke coming from the village of the Bear People and their other grandfather's home. Eventually their mother Rhpisunt became an old woman, and after she had died, they left the village, leaving their dog behind. They put on their bear coats when they reached the forest and

joined the Bear People. Ever after the tribe had good fortune when he reminded the Bear People that they were relatives and should help them with their hunting. All these events are believed to have happened at a village on the Nass River, and the story is owned by the people of the Wolf totem house.

Raven the Trickster

For some reason that is not quite clear many different peoples in the world have thought that the act of creation was some kind of trickery, and that the spirit who brought the world out of the waters had demonic qualities and a talent for deceit. This is faintly echoed in the story of Genesis, though here the serpent, rather than the

Creator, is the deceiver. But among primitive people the treachery of the Creator is always startlingly clear. From the tribes of the Northwest Coast of America the stories of the Trickster concern Raven. This remarkable personality brought man many of his most wonderful gifts, but he could never refrain from making fools of people.

Raven and the moon

One day Raven learnt that an old fisherman, living alone with his daughter on an island far to the north, had a box containing a bright light called the moon. He felt that he must get hold of this wonderful thing, so he changed himself into a leaf growing on a bush near to the old

fisherman's home. When the fisherman's daughter came to pick berries from the wild fruit patch, she pulled at the twig on which the leaf stood and it fell down and entered into her body. In time a child was born, a dark-complectioned boy with a long, hooked nose, almost like a bird's bill. As soon as the child could crawl, he began to cry for the moon. He would knock at the box and keep calling, 'Moon, moon, shining moon.'

At first nobody paid any attention, but as the child became more vocal and knocked harder at the box, the old fisherman said to his daughter, 'Well, perhaps we should give the boy the ball of light to play with.' The girl opened the box and took out another box, and then another, from inside that. All the boxes were beautifully painted and carved, and inside the tenth there was a net of nettle thread. She loosened this and opened the lid of the innermost box. Suddenly light filled the lodge, and they saw the moon inside the box, bright, round like a ball, shining white. The mother threw it towards her baby son and he caught and held it so firmly they thought he was content. But after a few days he began to fuss and cry again. His grandfather felt sorry for him and asked the mother to explain what the child was trying to say. So his mother listened very carefully and explained that he wanted to look out at the sky and see the stars in the dark

sky, but that the roof board over the smoke hole prevented him from doing so. So the old man said, 'Open the smoke hole.' No sooner had she opened the hole than the child changed himself back into the Raven. With the moon in his bill he flew off. After a moment he landed on a mountain top and then threw the moon into the sky where it remains, still circling in the heavens where Raven threw it.

Many of the stories about Raven describe his everyday adventures. Raven once met the wife of a fisherman. He had stuck a red robin feather in his head and this attracted her attention. She asked how she could get a red feather like that for her own hair. Raven said he could easily gets lots of them for her, so he and her husband went out to hunt for robins on an island. Raven rushed ahead of the fisherman and gathered pieces of rotten wood which he threw away among the trees, charming them so that they changed into robins. Then Raven showed the fisherman where to get the beautiful red birds, sending him deeper into the bush.

Raven then slipped away, hurried

to the canoe, paddled back to the shore, and turned himself into a man just like the fisherman. The fisherman's wife was quite sure that it was her husband who had returned home, so she was not surprised when he went straight to the special fishing pool where the finest fish were preserved and took some of them out to prepare himself a meal. As he finished eating, the fisherman returned saying that he had been fooled. He threw down the bagful of red feathers, which immediately changed back into a heap of rotten wood. He then chased Raven round the house, clubbing him into insensibility.

Then he threw away the body into the water. The drifting carcass was swallowed by a large halibut, but Raven resumed his own shape inside the halibut and so tormented it that it swam ashore, where a number of Indian fishermen seized it and began to cut it up and eat the delicious fat. To their astonishment Raven burst out of the fish and flew away. He screamed and cawed as ravens do, but the fishermen mistook it for profane language and were shocked. Raven

flew on and then alighted and changed himself into an old man and walked back to the shore. He could hear the fishermen talking about the foul bird that had slipped through their hands. He suddenly came among them and burst out laughing. 'I have now changed myself to an old man. I'm bent on destroying you unless you leave at once.' The whole tribe took to their heels, abandoning the village and all its food supplies to Raven.

The lady Hanging Hair

Some of the legends told by the Indians of northwest North America are surprisingly similar to those of ancient Europe. Here is one reminiscent of the story of Scylla and Charybdis. It tells of a dangerous whirlpool, Keagyihl Depguesk, which means 'Where it is turned upside down'. The people who lived in this particular region sorrowed when many of their bravest young men were sucked down into the waters.

Just across the river there lived a very gentle spirit whose name was Hanging Hair. She dwelt among the trees. When the wind blew the trees

Right. A grotesque mask in the form of a human face with a raven's mouth. It is surrounded by a ring of heads and may represent Raven and his other personalities. Museum of Mankind, London.

Opposite. Haida slate carving showing the pain suffered by Rhpisunt when she nursed one of her unnatural children. The projecting lower lip is caused by the insertion of a labret, or lip-plug. Smithsonian Institution, Washington, D.C. Bureau of American Ethnology.

Below. A ceremonial blanket of a Haida chief, from Prince of Wales Island, southeast Alaska, showing a bear outline made from shells. This picture emphasises its horrific aspect, but the Indians generally felt a sympathetic, if respectful, relationship to the bears.

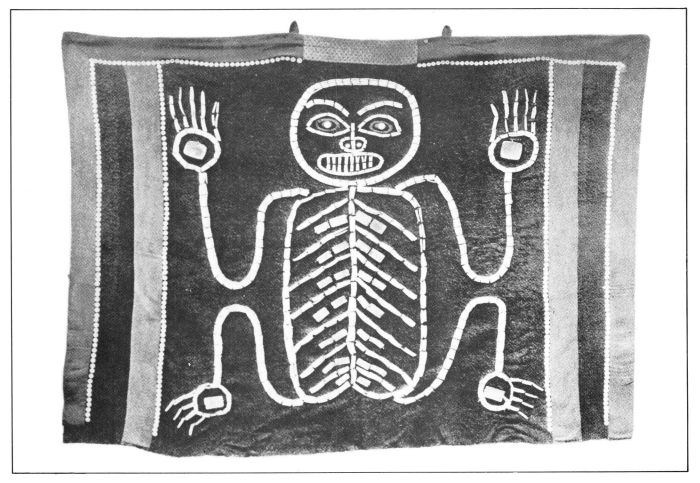

so that their branches swayed and hung down over the water, people thought that they could see this beautiful spirit. She protected those who lived nearby. It was she who called a great feast to arrange that Kaegyihl Depguesk should be disappointed of his prey. She invited all the monster powers of nature from the rivers and along the coast. Some of the guests came roaring along in a storm wind, others calm and gentle in the smooth water. Each one demonstrated his own particular skills; some falling as cliffs, some freezing as pieces of ice, some burning like forest fires, but all entering peacefully into the Festival House, which was under water.

Hanging Hair gave each one, even Kaegyihl Depguesk, his own place on the bench around the wall. Then from her store the hostess brought out the very precious and tasty kidney fat of mountain goats, placing some in front of each of the guests. By magic each piece became a large ball of the most perfect fat, and they ate of it until they were full. At the end of the feast, when everybody was in a good mood, the lady Hanging Hair said that it was time they should have more consideration for human beings, that people

who made offerings to the spirit of the whirlpool must not be cheated and destroyed, and that the powers of Kaegyihl Depguesk must be greatly reduced. Solemnly the monsters spoke in turn and finally agreed to shake the earth so that a high bluff, which deflected the water in the river, would be moved to another place, thus reducing the force of the water flowing through the whirlpool. When all the monsters were agreed, the earth shook, the wind blew and the forest fire burnt trees, but nobody in any of the villages was injured. When the storms had subsided, the high bluff had been broken down. The river was now quiet and broad, and the terrible whirlpool was no more than a gentle eddy that actually helped the fishermen on their way.

The Thunderbird

There are many stories of supernatural creatures. Some tell of the Thunderbird, an eagle with an extra head on its abdomen, which was powerful enough to carry off whales in its talons. Sometimes men actually saw the Thunderbird. One story tells of two hunters who travelled up a river until they arrived at a lake high in the mountains. They made their

camp and wrapped themselves for warmth in ferns and leaves. In the middle of the night they heard a tremendous noise coming from the lake. They looked into the water and there they saw an enormous bird. As it arose, a flash of lightning came from its beak and two children stood beside it. The monster bird spread its wings and the sound of them was a roaring of thunder, and lightning flashed again from its beak as it rose. Then it slowly sank back into the lake and when only the beak was visible it released another tremendous flash and roar. The local people, as well as the hunters, witnessed the scene, and feared for the men who were so close to the terrible bird. Their joy was great when they met the hunters unharmed. Together they returned to the village and rejoiced.

The fantastic worm

Other stories tell of dragon-like creatures. In some ways they resemble the Norse stories of huge and dreadful worms. One story from southern Alaska tells how a chief's daughter had a woodworm for a pet. She fed it with her own milk and as it grew bigger she took food for it from the storeboxes of her parents. When it

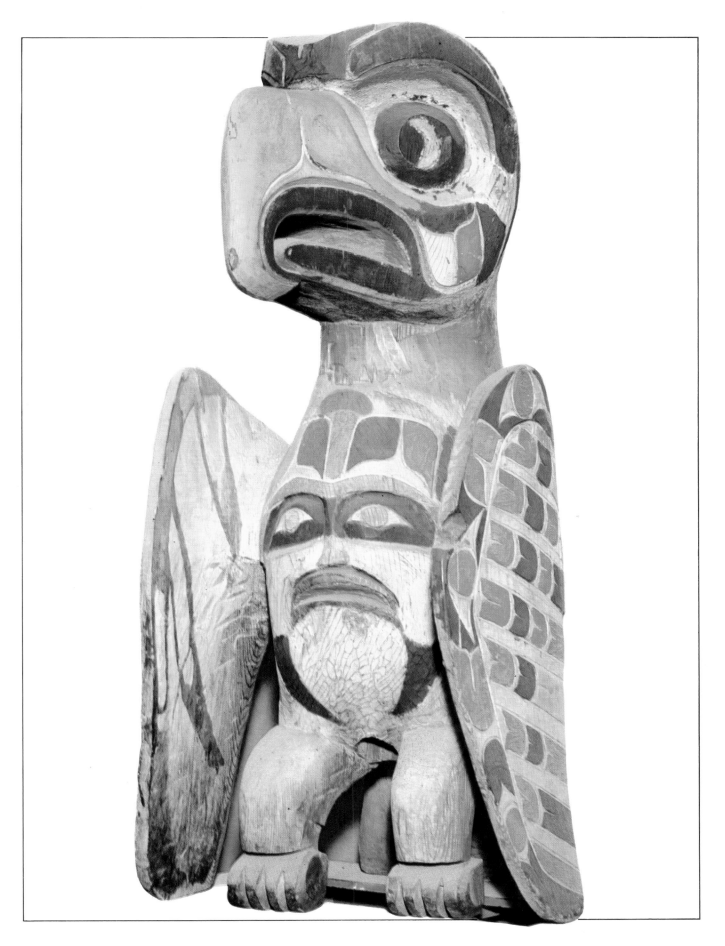

was two fathoms long she made up a cradle song for it, 'You have a face already and can sit up.' The words were repeated over and over again rhythmically. Later, as it grew, she sang, 'You have a mouth already. Sit right up.' Those who overheard these strange songs began to wonder what it was she sang to. The girl's mother peeped into the hut where, according to custom, the girl was secluded because of her first menstruation and saw the enormous worm. The people in the village were frightened, especially as some of them had noticed that the boxes in which they stored oil supplies for winter food had been emptied by some creature that tunnelled in underneath the ground. They blamed the worm.

The chief tried to persuade his daughter to come out of the seclusion hut and, knowing that she could not disobey, she changed her song into a mourning song for the worm and returned to her father's house. As soon as she had gone the villagers attacked the worm and cut it in pieces. The starvation that threatened them through the loss of their oil supplies was soon averted by good fortune and fishing. The girl explained that the tribe's success was due to the spirit of the worm and that it must now be regarded as a symbol of one of the totem clans of the Tlingit people.

The killer whales
In ancient times the greatest powers of the sea were the spirits of the killer whales. There is a heroic legend of a great hunter who met the killer whales in their enchanted home underneath the sea and still escaped.

The name of the hunter was Gunarhnesemgyet. Once he killed a white sea otter and skinned it. As he did so a little of the blood ran from the skin into the fur. He gave the skin to his wife to clean, and while she was busy washing it on the sea shore she happened to put both feet upon it and it drifted away. A large black whale came up and caught the skin on his back. The woman held on to his dorsal fin and cried out for help from the villagers, but the whale trav-

elled at tremendous speed and dived under the sea with her. Gunarhnesemgyet grabbed his hunting weapons ran to his canoe and with a friend, pursued the whale as fast as he could. He followed until he came to the place where the whale had dived. Here he took a long leather line, tied it to his boat and held on to it as he dived to the bottom of the ocean, where he found himself in another kind of world. He met a number of Cormorant People there, all blind. He approached them and cut their eyelids open so that they could see. In return they told him the way that he must travel. They warned him not to return by the same route but to follow a roundabout way to avoid capture.

Gunarhnesemgyet followed the trail that had been shown to him. He had gone some distance when he heard the sound of wood being chopped and saw a woodman who had broken the stone wedge that he used to split trees. He was weeping because his master, the Lord of the Killer Whales, would be angry with him. When Gunarhnesemgyet heard his story he put the wedge into his mouth, then took it out, blew upon it, made it whole and gave it back to the woodman. In return the woodman told him that he was cutting wood for Gunarhnesemgyet's wife who was building a fire inside the house of the killer whales. He also warned him that the whales would use magic to put a fin on her back so that she would become one of them. At Gunarhnesemgyet's request the woodman slipped several pails of water from the spring into the house. Gunarhnesemgyet hid near the door and pushed in a long stick and spilt the pails of water on to the hot stones

in the fireplace. Steam gushed from the fire and the house was filled with white mist. In the confusion Gunarhnesemgyet rushed to his wife crying, 'Come escape!' They made for the door. Gunarhnesemgyet put some magical medicine into his mouth and blew it towards the chief of the killer whales. The whale gradually began to swell, until he became so huge that he blocked the door. In an attempt to shrink him, his wives rushed over and urinated on him, but the shrinking was slow and it was some time before the whales could pass through the door. Thus Gunarhnesemgyet had a chance to escape with his wife. By the time the whales caught up with the pair they had reached the line attached to the canoe and had shaken it. Gunarhnesemgyet's companion felt the tug on the line and hauled up Gunarhnesemgyet and his wife. Meanwhile the Cormorant People had set traps into which they put a special herb which the killer whales swallowed and which put them to sleep. Gunarhnesemgyet and his wife threw out more of the magical herbs so as to delay the chase. Eventually they reached the safety of home, and the killer whales returned to their own world.

Mythical heroes

The story of the strong man with magic powers is another heroic myth found in every mythology. In European myths he is usually helped by gods or goddesses, but in the Northwest Coast stories the hero has a supernatural power within himself. Some of the stories concern Stoneribs, who was the son of Volcano Woman. It is said that as soon as he began to walk, he was able to make his own

Above. Tsimshian wooden shaman's puppet. Museum of the American Indian, Heye Foundation, New York.

Top. Kitksan 'soul-catcher, traditionally made from the femur of a bear. This was used by the shaman to trap the patient's soul during a healing ceremony, thereby aiding the cure. Lower Nass River, B.C. Museum of the American Indian, Heye Foundation, New York.

Opposite. Northwest-Coast rattle representing a bear and used to call up bears for the hunt. Museum of Mankind, London.

bow and arrow and shoot birds. Soon after his first adventures he heard voices crying in the winds. People farther to the south needed his help.

He left his mother and walked down to the seaside where he sat and watched the sea from underneath a cedar tree. An eagle flew across the water, seized a halibut and threw it on the beach. The boy picked up the flat fish and noticed that on its body there was a strip of copper, which he interpreted as a mark given to it specially by his mother, the Volcano Woman, for she had charge of all the copper in the world. He shot his arrow through the fish and tried to skin it, starting at the head and working towards the tail, but he was unable to do this. A voice from the cedar tree told him that he was working the wrong way. So he skinned the fish starting at the tail. Then he stretched out the skin to dry to make himself some clothing.

With the aid of the magical garment Stoneribs could turn himself into a supernatural being, able to swim in the sea like a halibut. In this disguise he swam rapidly southwards towards the voices crying for help. He came in to the shore, changed back into human form and crept through the bushes. He saw a canoe full of fishermen chased by finback whales which wrecked the canoe and killed the fishermen. He could still hear voices crying faintly for help and came to the village. There he saw a

Variations on a theme: *Above*. Beaver design on a Tsimshian dance apron, 19th century. Royal Scottish Museum, Edinburgh.

Right. Weaving a blanket with a similar striking design at present-day demonstration in British Columbia.

Opposite. Detail from box drum of the Haida Indians of the Northwest Coast. The design represents a bear, both quarry and protector in the mythology of the Haida. Field Museum of Natural History, Chicago, Illinois.

An ivory-headed shaman's rattle in the shape of a loon. The head on the bird's back represents its spirit. The loon features in Northwest-Coast mythology as a messenger from men to the world of spirits. Late 18th century, Vancouver Island, B.C. Museum of Mankind, London.

woman crying weakly, and with her was a baby screaming with hunger for there was no food. When he peeped into the house he saw only a few starving people lying about, unable to speak. He removed the child and took its place magically in the cradle. He gave unexpected power to the woman so that she could feed her new baby (Stoneribs) and he grew up magically to the full size of a man.

He want out to help the people collect some mussels for food. Before setting off in the canoe he took his bow and arrows, shot a blunt arrow at the side of the canoe and called out the name of the great sea monster 'Qagwaai' twelve times. Then, with the other tribesmen, he jumped into the canoe. Soon they saw the great sea monster, in the form of a killer whale, swimming after them with its mouth wide open. The boy took his arrow and shot at its head; it dived down, only to reappear and chase them again. Once more it opened its mouth ready to swallow them all, but the boy jumped into the gaping mouth and disappeared inside the

monster. As Qagwaai dived deep into the ocean, the boy wished for his magic power and then shot his arrow right through the monster, killing it from within. By killing Qagwaai Stoneribs punished the whales for killing so many tribesmen.

When the monster was cast up on the beach, the boy emerged, skinned it, and dried the skin in the sun. He put the skin over himself and was able to swim out to sea with the same power and speed as the dead monster.

He moved farther south to other islands, where he saw a great wooden house. Somebody within called out, 'Come, stay with me tonight.' He entered the house where he found a great monster. The monster gave him a box to lay his head on while he slept. As soon as his head touched it the box burst open. At this the monster realised that his visitor was something strange, and tried to trap him. It cried out 'Stone door, close yourself! Smoke hole, shut yourself!' And at once the house closed itself up. Stoneribs was trapped; he was still in the form of Qagwaai the whale, and

wondered how he could save himself within the space of a house that was only just big enough to hold him. He noticed that there was a narrow slit at the bottom of the stone door and remembered that he still had the halibut skin tied to his belt. He quickly put this on and the large and bulky whale was changed to a small flat halibut. Then he put his thin tail under the crack in the stone door and pushed. The stone shattered, salt water rushed into the house and he swam away.

Later he arrived safely at another inlet where he once more changed skins and became the magical whale. At the inlet, a gigantic crab spread out its legs to capture him. He was caught by one of its pinchers, which nearly squeezed him to death, even though he was in whale form. Again he put on the halibut skin and, again, suddenly reduced in size, slipped between the legs of the crab and escaped leaving the large whale skin in the trap. Disguised as a halibut he swam on and eventually managed to come up in a safe bay where he took

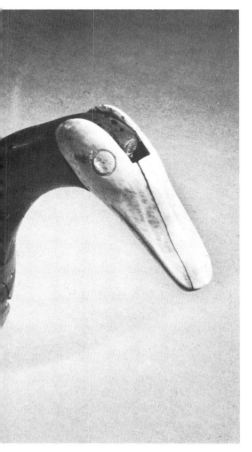

his halibut skin off and hung it up to dry while he sat down warming himself in the sun. Suddenly he heard a noise and was just in time to see an eagle steal his halibut skin and fly away with it. He called other birds to attack the eagle, but he heard a voice from the woods telling him that he must not touch the eagle, that the skin had only been lent and now it had been taken away as magically as it had come. So he decided to travel no more and returned in his normal human form to his mother. Proud of her courageous son she gave him a new name; instead of Stoneribs he was ever after called Crystalribs.

The lazy boy

There are many other tales told of mystical heroes with spiritual power that gave them the ability to overcome natural obstacles. One young boy was a lazy and over-sleepy child, and everybody called him names and laughed at him. When the men were away hunting or fishing he would go to the sea and wash himself with magical herbs so that he became stronger and stronger in secret. But whenever other people were near he would pretend to be as lazy and foolish as usual. Whenever trouble came to the tribe they always left him to the very last before asking him for help. When they did ask, however, he had such strength that people soon realised that he was not lazy and foolish but that he was a supernatural being.

As time passed, the world seemed to threaten the tribespeople and they did not know what to do. The forest trees and the mountains slowly moved in, crushing the settlements, driving people away, killing them. The chiefs and magicians all tried their magic powers, but without success. Finally the people decided that the only thing to do was to abandon their homes and crowd themselves into the canoes and get away to sea. Just as they were stepping into the last canoe the young hero awoke from his sleep in the corner and said, 'Why is everybody so excited? Why are they going away?' The chief replied, 'If you

Above. Chief holding a ceremonial copper, *c.* 1895. Smithsonian Institution, Washington, D.C.

could keep awake you'd know that the forest is pushing us into the sea. Whole villages have vanished while you slept.'

The young man then rose up and went to the back of the house. There he began to pull up trees, roots and all, to build a barricade. He pushed it forwards, sweeping the entire forest back into the hills. He kept on pulling up trees by the roots, and so made it forever impossible for the forest to move again. He returned to the village and said to the people, 'It is well that you have only little things like this to worry you.' And without another word he curled up on a warm bed near the fire and slept again as though he had never been disturbed. Soon after this, the spirits who control the shape of the earth started flattening the hills. Once again the people prepared to run away, but first they told the young man. He was quite unconcerned and went to sleep again, but when the people's fears grew he took action. First he chewed some of his magical herbs and bathed, then he called the loon bird to his aid. He said, 'Go to my grandfather and tell him what is happening. I must help the people. I must push the mountains and hills back and divide them, so that the rivers can flow through them.' At once the bird flew off with the message. When, later on, the young man heard the loon calling him he knew that his grandfather had sent him the magical powers he needed. He threw back the hills and the mountains, and broke them apart, so that rivers ran between them and it was no longer possible for them to cascade down bringing destruction. Then he returned to his uncle's house, lay down and fell asleep.

The people acclaimed and feared him as the greatest of all magicians and medicine men. But one night a large canoe landed and a man disembarked with his servants, saying, 'This is the place where our master sleeps. We are seeking him.' They walked straight to the chief's house where the young man lay. They said, 'Master, great chief, your grandfather is ill and sent us. You have done everything that can be done. Your

mission is finished. Your canoe is waiting.' He answered and said, 'I am ready.' Then he turned to the chief and said, 'I must go to my grandfather who has grown weak. I must relieve him of his work of holding up the earth on a long pole. Now I shall hold it in his place. But remember, never ridicule somebody you do not know. Now you can rest assured that no more harm will befall the world.' And he joined his strange visitors.

Now whenever the young man spreads his arms or moves his feet he causes earthquakes and when the medicine men wish to send a message to him the loon is his messenger.

The myths of the Northwest Coast Indians are influenced by the dominating features of their lives. Thus the salmon and bears which are important food animals to the tribes play a part in their myths and have spirits that have to be placated. Other creatures, dangerous to man, such as the eagle and the whale, are feared for their supernatural powers as well as their physical powers. Parallel to the stories of the supernatural monsters are stories of the mythical hero with supernatural powers of his own, who can oppose them on equal terms. In their emphasis on force and cunning, all these myths reflect the aggressive life of tribes of this region who depended on hunting.

The Hunters of the Northern Forests

In the parts of North America that were too cold to support maize there were hunting tribes who moved continuously among the forests hunting for deer and beaver. During the long, snow-bound winters they relied for food on fishing through holes in river ice, scouting for hibernating bears and digging out beaver lodges. In addition they had supplies of pemmican, a thick pastry substance which they made in autumn by pounding dried meat with caribou fat and nourishing berries, and which could be preserved almost indefinitely in birch-bark containers.

In the summer the forests teemed with life. Rivers could be navigated in birch-bark canoes that were used more for fishing than as a means of transport, although tribal territory sometimes extended over some hundreds of miles. In this land then, there were small communities of several families travelling over their hunting territories and occasionally meeting together for ceremonial occasions. Their clothing was made entirely from skins, and covered them completely as a protection against the cold of winter and the attacks of the mosquitos in the summer. No half-naked tribe would have been able to survive in these conditions.

The Cree

These Indians of the Northern forests were mostly members of the great Cree nation, divided into widely separated bands, but all speaking a common language. In earlier times their culture was based on the possession of good, flaked-stone tools. They used arrow heads, scrapers and knives, but as they had no need to cut down trees they never invented heavy stone axes. The forest itself was a home in which both the hunter and the hunted lived with some degree of comfort. The number of animals, though quite large, was not sufficient to support a settled population. The hunters added to their diet all kinds of wild berries, and some of the grasses produced edible

grain which was beaten to make paste, or boiled for gruel.

Ancestor spirits

The mythology of the Cree people was based on the spirits of the hunt. They believed in an earth spirit who was mother of the animals; and in an ill-defined sky being who displayed a general interest in the human race. But the root of their religion lay in their close relationship with their ancestors. It was felt that the 'old people' were always near, ready to assist the tribe with advice or warning. Occasionally, people who were endowed with shamanistic faculties would fall into a trance and

The great northern forests teemed with life. The hunting tribes moved among the forests - sometimes over great distances – fishing and hunting for deer, beaver, bears and other wild life.

visit the camps of the ancestors underneath the earth. But as in most legends of this kind, it was emphasised that the visitor should accept no hospitality at the hands of his hosts. Once the food of the dead had been eaten by a living man, his spirit was captured by its new environment and his body, lying in trance in the upper earth, simply died.

The movements of the forest people were dependent upon the seasons and they had many legends about the winds and about the positions of the sun and stars. As is usual in such a mythology the animals could speak and tell stories, for the whole of nature was an integrated community of animals and men. The world of the primitive hunter was extremely limited, not only in its human contact but also in the development of myths

and stories. The relationship between the family and the spirit world was as simple as its relationship with the other families who made up the small tribal group.

The development of more complex beliefs came from contact with more advanced people, or from the adoption of an agricultural routine. This step forward was a vital one in all human societies. Its importance is observed, for example, in the biblical story of Cain and Abel, where the favoured brother was the one who made offerings of the fruits of agriculture rather than those of hunting. Once men learnt to dig the earth in order to grow grain, they took on a completely new relationship with the world of nature, and from this new relationship a new body of myths evolved.

Fertility spirits

The new mythology centred around the fertility spirits, who were often a group of goddesses who in many ways mirrored the development of a woman's life. Not surprisingly they were often linked with the monthly phases of the moon. The idea of a protective old father also begins to appear, although in North America this was never a very clearly defined concept. The Great Spirit was a vague

generality, a being who did not have contact directly with the shaman but who was known to preside over the activities of the forces of nature. These forces were imminent everywhere; as thunder and hail they had the power to destroy the crops and so reduce man to starvation; as warm winds and rains in the right season they brought blessings. For the primitive agriculturist, closer observation of nature became important.

Myths of stars and seasons

Because crops maturing at different seasons demand a much more complex knowledge of the calendar than is found among simple hunting peoples. Astronomical myths also become more numerous and detailed. The development of agriculture is therefore accompanied by a tendency to divide the sky into regions in which the sun and the planets would appear at different seasons of the year. This in its turn leads to a mythology based on the inter-relations of the planets and their special influences as they move from one part of the heavens to another. There is also a much more complex mythology about rainbows, clouds and thunderstorms.

For example, among the Algonquin tribes there was the cycle of legends which Longfellow described in his

Above. Caribou mask from the Winter Solstice ceremony. Naskapi, Labrador. Museum of the American Indian, Heye Foundation, New York.

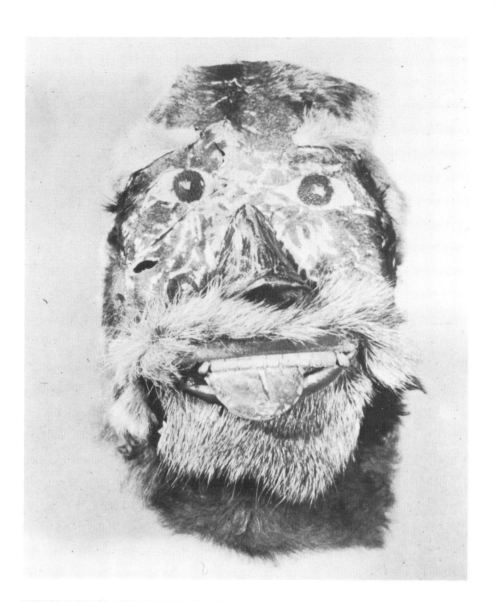

Right. A wooden box in which the eagle feather headdress of a Ojibwa Indian was stored in between ceremonies. The lid bears a pictograph record of one of the ceremonial chants and could only be read by an initiate. Wisconsin, 1850–75. Museum of the American Indian, Heye Foundation, New York.

Song of Hiawatha. (The name Hiawatha was wrongly used as it was actually the name of an Iroquois chief who was one of the founders of the Five Nations.) This cycle of stories represents the generalised mythology of an Algonquin group who had rudimentary agriculture but still lived largely by hunting. Their social structure was reflected very clearly in the myths, and there was also a very strong emphasis on the rhythms of the seasons. But the break with the simple hunting mythology of tribes like the Cree was by no means complete. Ancient traditions lingered on among the agriculturists, and remained a strong influence among those tribes who still subsisted largely by hunting.

Village festivals

The new agricultural life was accompanied by greater sophistication in the stories, since they were no longer mere anecdotes recited among members of the family, but began to form part of the oral literature of large communities when settled villages became possible. In the North American forest climate villages usually had two sites, one for winter living, the other for summer living. On moving from one site to another the whole community would have a few days of festival in which

stories were told and myths enacted before an audience often of more than 1,000 people. On the great occasions when tribal meetings brought people from several villages, it was not impossible for as many as 7,000 or 8,000 people to come together. The stories began to assume definite epic form, to which recognisable heroic archetypes went through a series of adventures. The mythological epics of the farming tribes are completely distinct from the more primitive stories, which have one or two episodes of an emotional character but no continuous theme.

The figure of the deceiver, who is also a culture-bringer and a creator, is a common one in North American mythology. The figure varies considerably in psychological significance, sometimes suggesting merely the spirit of uncertainty (like the Fool in the pack of Tarot cards), in other forms suggesting a strong demonic power more like the terrible Mexican deity Tezcatlipoca. This first story comes from the Eastern Cree Indians.

Wisagatcak and the creation of the world

The Trickster Wisagatcak built a dam of stakes across a creek in order to trap the Giant Beaver when it swam out of its lodge. He waited all day, until in the evening he saw the creature swimming towards him. He was ready to spear it, when Muskrat suddenly bit him from behind and made his spear stroke miss. So he gave up hunting that night. Next morning he decided to break down the dam, so he levered the stakes of the dam out of place. The water flowed out, and kept on flowing. But the level of the creek did not fall. The Giant Beavers had worked magic against Wisagatcak because he had broken the dam. All the land was covered. As the waters rose Wisagatcak pulled up some trees to make a raft and collected many different kinds of animals which were swimming about in the waters. For two weeks the Beavers made the waters rise until no land was left. At the end of the two weeks Muskrat left the raft and dived down but could

not find any earth, and stayed below the surface so long that he died. Then Raven left the raft; he flew for a whole day yet saw no land, only water in all the four directions. Then Wisagatcak made his own magic and called Wolf to help. Wolf ran round and round the raft with a ball of moss in his mouth. As he ran, the moss grew and earth formed on it. Then he put it down and they danced around it singing powerful spells. The earth grew. It spread over the raft and went on growing until it made the whole world. The Cree storytellers enforce this myth by pointing out how sometimes the water that is now beneath the earth pours out as a spring from under the rocks.

The brothers who created the world

The Algonquin creation myth is more sophisticated. The general form approaches that of the Iroquois legends in that it describes a duality. In this case the creator force was Gluskap, who had a destructive wolf-brother Malsum. When their creator died, Malsum made rocks, thickets and poisonous animals, while Gluskap took the body of this mother earth to form the pleasant plains, the food plants, animals, and the human race. Malsum tried to find out what magic could kill his rival, and in jest asked him what could kill him, adding that only fern root could cause his own death. Gluskap replied that an owl feather was the only thing that could slay him. So one evening Malsum took the feather of an owl's wing and used it in place of an arrow head to shoot his brother. Gluskap fell dead but immediately after, by his great magic, he recovered. Suspecting his brother's treachery he went into the forest and sat by a stream declaring that only a flowering reed would kill him. A toad hearing this hopped away and told Malsum the secret, asking for the power to fly as a reward. But Malsum refused to give the toad the power of flight, and said it would look silly with wings. To be revenged the creature hurried back to Gluskap and told him of his danger. Gluskap thereupon plucked a large-rooted fern stem. With it he struck

Above. Bag of beadwork and wool yarn woven by the Sauk and Fox Indians in the Underwater Panther design, *c.* 1880. The design symbolised one of the origin myths of the Great Lakes Tribes. Detroit Institute of Arts, Michigan.

Opposite. The Ojibwa Snowshoe Dance was performed to thank the Great Spirit for sending the first snow of the winter. Thick snow made it easier for the hunters to chase game on their snowshoes. Museum of Mankind, London.

down Malsum and killed him, driving his evil magic below the earth. Unlike his brother, Malsum was unable to revive; he became a cruel and vindictive wolf. (Since the Algonquin Indians were trading with the Norse Vinlanders for four centuries and more before Columbus, this story possibly has some echoes of Norse mythology.)

Left in peace Gluskap completed the creation of the world from the body of his mother. He drove away many evil creatures and conquered the stone giants. But he was often of a whimsical turn of mind. In one case, when four men came to him begging that he would help them, he asked them what they wished. One wanted to become gentle instead of quarrelsome, another wished for enough riches to get himself a home and not be a despised beggar, a third, who was laughed at by the tribe, wanted to become an ordinary man, as stately and respected as his fellows. The fourth wanted to be taller and more beautiful than other men so that he could rule over everyone. So Gluskap gave each a box of medicine. The first three found it gave them their wishes; and so did the fourth – he grew tall and stately and spread his arms, and arms, and more arms – for he was the first and greatest of all pine trees.

Gluskap had one fault: pride. He had done such wonderful things and conquered so much evil that he would not believe that anyone could defeat him. But one day a poor woman told him that she knew one person who could withstand all his powers. He refused to believe her, but she persuaded him to come into her bark lodge. Making himself as small as an ordinary man, he entered. There, sitting on the floor newly dusted with white ashes, was a baby boy. The great Gluskap sang and the child

smiled. He told it to walk, still the child only smiled. He changed himself into strange shapes and the child laughed happily, but it would neither walk nor talk with him. He grew angry and shouted, whereupon the child burst into tears, but still neither walked nor talked. The great wonder-worker was defeated.

Eventually Gluskap left the land in a birch-bark canoe, travelling towards the sunrise, for his work was completed, but it was believed he might return one day.

The myths of the forest Indians show the development of a more sophisticated mythology as the tribes turn from a life of hunting to an agricultural routine. The transition can be seen in the story of Wisagatcak, where a typical hunting myth about a man being punished by the spirits for his ill-treatment of animals develops into the story of creation. The growth of large settled communities made possible regular tribal festivals which gave rise to the epic legend in which a hero, such as Gluskap,

goes through a series of adventures. This transition from hunting to agricultural preoccupations, which is evident in the myths of the Northern Forests, is almost complete in the Eastern Woodlands.

The Farmers of the Eastern Woodlands

The Indian peoples south of the St Lawrence River down to Delaware Bay, and inland to the region of the Great Lakes, were grouped in many tribes, speaking three main languages. Most of them were members of the Iroquois people, known as the Five Nations. Like their southern neighbours, the Delaware, and their northern neighbours, the Algonquin tribes, they inhabited a temperate woodland country where the heavy snows of winter were followed by warm moist summers – in other words, the climate of New York today.

These groups of Indians have altered so much in their centuries of close contact with Europeans that it is difficult to discover much about their earlier life. The first objective accounts of them come a century after the first white settlements. They appear to have had a mixed economy when first discovered by the white man. The rivers and lakes provided good fishing and there was much hunting for deer and moose, as well as for the fur-bearing animals such as beaver, squirrel and fox. In addition, they all had a good knowledge of agriculture, based mainly on the cultivation of maize, which had spread, over a very long period of time, from the Mexican plateau through the American southwest, proceeding mostly by trade and barter along the rivers until it reached the region of the Eastern Woodlands. Agricultural techniques were fairly simple. Hoes and digging sticks were used to break the ground, and the earth was piled up into small hillocks in which maize seeds were planted. Fields were carefully weeded and tended by the women and children. After a few years a field would be abandoned and another piece of land cleared while the original area lay fallow. It was rapidly covered by scrubby undergrowth and remained fallow sometimes for fifteen or twenty years.

Indian villages, set among their fields and protected by a stockade, were made up of a number of longhouses, each of which consisted of a framework of bent saplings built in the form of a row of arches, sometimes fifteen or twenty feet (four to six metres) high and twenty feet wide at the base. This arched structure was covered with sheets of birch and elmbark to make a weatherproof covering. Screens divided the longhouse interior into family apartments, each with its own fireplace and smokehole in the roof. A large village might consist of three or four longhouses each over a hundred feet long.

Transport was primitive, since the horse was not introduced until after the settlement of North America by Europeans. People travelled on foot with packs on their backs, but by far the most popular form of travel was by birchbark canoe. These light canoes, which could easily be carried by one person, were ideally suited to the mountainous forest country. It was often necessary to leave one river system and carry the boat across to another group of rivers in order to travel from one important village to another. It was possible for most of the crew to step out and carry the

The Indians of the Eastern Woodlands had a wide knowledge of agriculture at the time of discovery by Europeans. Agricultural festivals were held six times a year at which braided cornhusk masks such as this Iroquois one were worn. New York State Museum, Albany.

load in bundles on their backs, while the canoe itself was carried to the next river and prepared for reloading at a landing stage.

The Indians' basic tools were made of stone until after contact with Europeans. They did much woodcarving, of which very little has survived, but what remains is pleasant in its simplification of natural form. They wore less clothing than in historic times. Leggings, breech clout and cape formed the costume of the men. Women wore knee-length skirts to which was added a large skin cloak in bad weather. It is difficult, in view of the almost complete lack of archaeological material, to know much about the daily life. More of it is preserved in folk lore than in any other way. But probably the social organisation has been preserved carefully because tradition in tribal life was always important.

Wampum belts

Records of tribal history and remarkable adventures were kept through a system of mnemonic objects. These were usually strings or belts of wampum, made of large numbers of cylindrical beads of white and purple shell. Wampum was a valuable article of exchange, and a fathom, that is a string of wampum as long as a man's arm-span, was a unit of value recognised over the tribal territories of the northeastern region.

Keepers of the Wampum were important tribal dignitaries, who kept the store of historic strings and belts in special wooden boxes. At the great annual tribal gatherings the belts were brought out and the stories associated with them recited to the people, so that everyone should be acquainted with tribal history and tradition. Young men who showed

Hiawatha and the Five Nations

The Iroquois were an important people because they built up a tribal federation which united five separate Indian nations (the Seneca, Cayuga, Onondaga, Oneida and Mohawk), all speaking the same basic language, who had previously been constantly at war. This union, formed in the 16th century as a response to the depredations of Algonquin neighbours, was brought about by a chief of the Mohawk tribe. He was invited to the Council of Hereditary Chiefs because of his intellectual distinction, and was appointed one of the Lone Pine chieftains who were chosen from among respected tribal members regardless of their family. His name was *Haio hwa tha*, pronounced Hiawatha by the white men. He was able to convince the Council that if Indian life were to continue, the bitter and murderous wars between the five Iroquois tribes must be replaced by federation and regular meetings for united ceremonies. They must prepare plans for spreading the confederation further and further from tribe to tribe until, one day, they would unite all the Indian nations of North America. However, this was not to be; they became involved in the wars between the French and the English and their own tribal organisation was badly undermined, although ceremonial meetings, their system of chieftainship and, above all, their great respect for the powers of nature, all continue down to the present day.

It is plain that the Iroquois plan was a piece of advanced political thinking. In practice it developed as an organisation for allowing crops to be grown in peace and for organising tribal wars far from their own territory so that no harm could come to the Iroquois people. On one occasion they even raided the Black Hills of Dakota. From this region, 1,000 miles (1,600 kilometres) from their homeland, they carried prisoners tied on their backs. They were brought back to the great festival so that they could be tortured to death in the ceremonial of fire, by which they were burnt in various parts of their bodies,

Above. A Seneca False Face mask, known as a 'Speaker Mask'. It was worn at the ceremonies held to drive away False Face spirits from the tribes. Museum of the American Indian, Heye Foundation, New York.

promise were taken on to be servants and assistants to the Keepers of the Wampum, so that they might learn the tradition more thoroughly and, in time, take over the great responsibility of preserving the unity of the tribe through its historic past.

Most of the Iroquois myths that we now know were first recorded by missionaries and traders in the late 17th and 18th centuries and we have no real check on their earlier forms. The custom of holding faithfully to tradition can be assumed to have existed among the Iroquois long before the arrival of Europeans.

Above left. The rivers and lakes of the Eastern Woodlands provided good fishing, and in the forests were moose and deer, and fur-bearing animals such as beaver, squirrel and fox. The Indians of the Eastern Woodlands had a mixed economy, in which agriculture also played an important role.

63

A village of wigwams drawn in the early 16th century by one of the first European visitors, John White. A framework of arched saplings was covered with birch or elmbark to make a permanent dwelling for one or more families. Museum of Mankind, London.

for a day or more. It was considered a matter of great importance for a prisoner to be able to show no fear of pain, and to continue singing his death song, praising his own bravery and reviling his captors, until he finally became unconscious. This practice, like the hunting of scalps, was fairly widespread in ancient North America, although there is some reason to think that it grew worse when the European powers recruited Indians as allies in their own struggles to achieve domination of the Continent.

The supreme spirit

Religion among the Indian tribes of the Eastern Woodlands is reported to include the concept of an All-Father of the type of Odin or Zeus, but it is possible that this concept derived from contact with European Christians, which began with the visit of the Norse Vinlanders in the early 11th century. The concept, found among the Northwest Coast Indians, of a sky house where an angry old chief lived, was no doubt an explanation of meteorological phenomena. The Indians of the great forests, however, had a wider concept of nature and their thinkers postulated a supreme spirit, all-embracing, but without form and having little contact with men. The concept was more like an abstract notion, such as Time, thought of as the bearer of foreordained events. For most people this Great Spirit, *Ha wen neyu*, was an ever present emotive force which took second place to the world of nature spirits who were more concerned with daily events.

Iroquois beliefs

The whole world seemed imbued with life to the primitive agriculturalists. The Iroquois and their kindred tribes knew of the spirit forces which drove rivers, danced with the rain clouds, swept through the trees, and changed the face of the land in spring and autumn. The food crops were blessed by protective spirits, the three sisters, sometimes glimpsed as they rustled among the corn or shook the stems of the squash or pumpkin.

The religious life of these tribes was much more organised than that of the hunting tribes. It centred very largely around shamanistic practices where the usual accompaniment of dance, song and trance were to be observed. But there was also a highly organised theology. The concept of supreme power among the Iroquois was expressed in the idea that all existence was a struggle between the duality of light and darkness, of good and misfortune. The concept of evil, as we know it, is not characteristic of primitive religion in any part of the world. What was called bad meant that which was unlucky in material affairs.

The passage of the seasons and the growth of crops made the people aware of the importance of the calendar. Great respect was paid to the sun, moon and stars; in particular, the Morning Star was very important. As among all American Indians, the four directions – north, south, east and west – were important to their beliefs. In many of the legends, spirits behave in different ways according to which of the four regions their activities took place in. The universe was believed to be directed by spiritual powers of a mysterious nature to whom men must constantly pray for assistance and guidance. Offerings must be made to the first of the harvest, for example, and certain portions of hunted animals. In general human sacrifice was rare except for the prestige killing of prisoners.

The Iroquois believed that there was a land of the dead somewhere far away. Warrior spirits in particular were thought to inhabit the sky, and some stories associate them with the appearance of aurora borealis in the northern heavens. There was also an underworld Mother of Animals and, of course, a great number of ancestral spirits. Not only did the ancestors watch over men in their daily activities, but they could also be visited in dreams, when they would be found living in beautiful villages underneath the earth, in a condition which seems to have been rather better than that of life on the surface. There was

neither war nor sickness, and they never lacked skins or food.

Agricultural festivals

As elsewhere, agricultural life here demanded a different rhythm from hunting. The hunters' two seasons of animal migration were replaced among the Iroquois with six regular festivals based on the stages of plant growth – the Maple Festival, held in the spring to celebrate the rising of the maple sap (an important food item); the Planting Festival to seek blessing on the seed; the Wild Strawberry Festival to give thanks for the first wild fruits; the Green Corn Festival to celebrate the ripening of the maize, beans and squash; the Harvest Festival; and the Midwinter or New Year Festival. At the last-named festival, the longest and most important ceremonies were held. It involved a cleansing ritual in which public confessions of the past year's misdeeds and evil thoughts were

made while holding a belt of white wampum. Sometimes people tickled their throats with wooden sticks until they vomited, thus cleansing themselves in preparation for the new agricultural year about to begin. Thanks were expressed to the Great Spirit and, in early times, a white dog was sometimes sacrificed and sent to the skies as a messenger.

Thus at every stage of the ritual year there was a reminder of the relationship between the spirit world and human beings. The festivals were always great social occasions, with a good deal of jollification, but the ceremonies were very serious. Even the wild behaviour of the masked performers of the False-Face Society had a serious purpose in seeking, through their rituals, to cure and prevent disease, both in individuals and in the community as a whole. Another was the Husk-Face Society, whose members wore masks made of plaited coils of maize husks.

In this outward expression of the myths there are parallels with the agricultural rituals of Europe which are very striking, and which include carnivals, masked begging by children and mummers plays. Man has a tendency to develop a sympathetic magical relationship with nature, and to mime and mask the desired events. Since agricultural pursuits are so closely linked with fertility and the wonders of sex, the festivals were often occasions of free and happy licence, without the usual social inhibitions. This part of the celebrations has persisted through time, even after the close link between human behaviour and favourable harvests has been abandoned as an article of faith.

Because of the long contact between the Iroquois and European missionaries and traders, it is probably best to study the myths of these woodland Indians through the stories of the less acculturised people such as the Hurons, who never amalga-

Seneca Iroquois 'Crooked Mouth' mask, False Face Society. New York. Museum of the American Indian, Heye Foundation, New York.

mated in the Iroquois manner. The following is a creation legend reported in earlier times from the Iroquois as well as more recently from Huron and Wyandot story-tellers.

The creation of the world

The first people lived beyond the sky because there was no earth beneath. The chief's daughter fell ill and no cure could be found. A wise old man was consulted and he told them to dig up a tree and lay the girl beside the hole. Many people began to dig but as they did so the tree suddenly fell right through the hole they had made dragging the girl with it.

Below was an endless sheet of water where two swans floated. There was a sound, the first thunder clap, and as the swans looked up, they saw the sky break and a strange tree fall down into the water. Then they saw the girl fall after it. They swam to her and supported her because she was too beautiful to allow to drown. Then they swam to the Great Turtle, master of all the animals, who at once called a council.

When all the animals had arrived the Great Turtle told them that the appearance of a woman from the sky foreshadowed future good fortune. Since the tree had earth on its roots, he commanded them to find where it had sunk, and then to bring up some of the earth, so that it could be put on his back to make an island for the woman to live upon.

The swans led the animals to the place where the tree had fallen. First Otter, then Muskrat and then Beaver dived. As each one came up from the great depths he rolled over exhausted and died. Many other animals tried but the same fate overcame them. At last the old lady Toad volunteered. She had been below a long time, until all the animals thought she had been lost, when at last she surfaced and before dying managed to spit a mouthful of earth on the back of the Great Turtle. It was magical earth and had the power of growth. As soon as it was as big as an island the woman was set down upon it. The two white swans circled it, and it

continued to grow, until at last it became the world island as it is today, supported in the great waters on the back of the Turtle. But it was dark. Again the Great Turtle called the animals. They pondered for a long time. They decided they should put a great light in the sky. But no one could take it there, until the Great Turtle called Little Turtle and she confessed that she might be able to climb the dangerous path to the heavens. Everyone invoked their own magical powers to assist her. A great black cloud was formed; it was full of clashing rocks, and from their movement lightning flashed out. Little Turtle climbed into this cloud and was carried around the sky, collecting the lightning as she went. First she made a big bright ball of it and threw it into the sky. Then she thought it was well to have some more light so she collected still more lightning but only enough for a smaller ball. The first ball became the sun, and the second the moon. Then the Great Turtle commanded the burrowing animals to make holes in the corners of the sky so that the sun and moon could go down through one and climb up again through the other as they circled. So there was day and night.

Astronomical myths

The sun and moon were credited with human words and deeds. They quarrelled. They were like man and wife. Once the moon passed through the hole at the edge of the sky before her husband. He was enraged and beat her so violently that she disappeared for a time. Again Little Turtle set off, this time into the dark world below. There she found the Moon Woman who had lost most of her light because she had pined away. She was so thin that instead of a ball she was only a tiny crescent. Little Turtle mended the moon and set her on her course again. She gradually became her own round self; but as the sun passed in the opposite direction he looked away and refused to recognise her. Again she began to pine away. And so it has continued ever since, with the moon hoping and sorrowing

each time she passes round her cycle with the sun.

It was after this that the thunder cloud came down and the rain made a rainbow. The deer saw this wonderful bridge and raced up its shining pathway to find a pasture in the sky. Later Little Turtle found that the other animals envied the deer, and allowed many of them to climb the rainbow. They can now be seen as the stars.

This composite legend continues with the birth of the two opposing gods on earth. The idea of a Spirit of Blessing and a cruel Trickster is very common in North American Indian mythology. It is almost certainly derived from ancient tradition and the beings are, in fact, archetypal figures derived from certain aspects of the unconscious mind. The Wyandot version described here divides the whole world into pleasant and easy, and unpleasant and difficult. This division is only part of the concept however. Further study reveals that the two opposing principles are creative usefulness and harsh destructiveness. To find that the destructive force was reckoned the less powerful by these simple farming tribespeople comes as a slight surprise.

The destructive and creative twins

When the Woman Fallen from the Sky was settled on the world island, she realised that she was pregnant with twins, one of whom, Taweskare, said he would kick his way through

his mother's side. Tsentsa, the other twin, told him he was evil, and that they should be born in the usual way. The Woman had found her mother, who also descended from the sky to help her. But when the time came the evil twin burst forth from his mother's armpit and so killed her. The little boys, however, were strong and healthy and were brought up by their grandmother.

It was the gentle Tsentsa's habit to work for a while and then rest. While he was resting Taweskare would work even harder undoing the good that his brother had wrought. When the fertile plains and undulating valleys were made on the world island, Taweskare heaved parts of them up to make barren mountains, and cleft others to make terrible chasms and swamps. The good power made a world of fruit trees and pleasant bushes; the evil one made the fruit small and gritty and put thorns on the bushes. One made fishes smooth, the other covered them with horny scales. For long ages the struggle continued and later legend shows the evil twin retreating west to create the terrible Rocky Mountains.

The atmospheric powers

The twins Tsentsa and Taweskare had shaped the earth. The powers of nature who succeeded them were very close to man. One of the great seasonal powers was the Thunder. Thunder marked the atmospheric changes which heralded the coming of spring, and basically the farming

Above. Although primarily an agricultural people, the Eastern Woodlands tribes still depended on hunting for their meat. This mask is made from the head of a deer and was worn at ceremonies designed to bring better hunting to the tribe. Nationalmuseet, Copenhagen.

Top, left. Records of tribal history were kept through mnemonic objects, usually strings of wampum beads. A wampum belt would be carried over the arm of the Keeper of the Wampum at the great festivals and the stories connected with it recited to the people. This one has a medicine bag attached in the form of a turtle – the animal which was believed to support the world. Museum of Mankind, London.

Top, right. The Iroquois believed that food crops were blessed by protective feminine spirits. This watercolour showing the Corn, Bean and Squash Maidens was painted by a Seneca Indian artist, Ernest Smith, in the 1930s. Rochester Museum of Arts and Sciences, New York.

Opposite. False Face 'Harvest' mask, *c*. 1870. Onondaga Iroquois, New York State. Museum of the American Indian, Heye Foundation, New York.

tribes thought of Thunder as showering blessings. But sometimes Thunder swept in bringing destruction and danger, so they assumed a family of thunder children less responsible than the parent. Herein were the seeds of the highly developed mythology of the rain and lightning spirits of Middle North American civilisations. In some ways it recalls the cults of Thor Red-Beard and Jupiter Tonans in Europe. But the woodland Indians took a simpler attitude than the Europeans. They lived close to nature, had no temples, and included Thunder among the Manitous or spirits who were given offerings of prayer and dance at the seasonal festivals.

Thunder was one of seven brothers. He was named Heng, a big, vigorous youngster and a great favourite with the others in spite of the unfortunate clumsiness which caused him to break everything he touched. But in the end Heng's clumsy behaviour so exhausted his brothers that they had to part from him. They took him to an island in a mountain lake. Then they slipped away taking his canoe with them. At first Heng was very angry and stormed terribly, but in time he found his island so pleasant that he made it his home.

Earth and sky spirits

Thunder is a sky power and therefore different from the powers of the earth and underworld. The following myth describes the antagonism at work between the forces above and below, and the feminine force of the earth surface. Part of it derives from simple meteorological observation. The Indians had noticed that lightning was like a serpent, striking both downwards and upwards, and that plants after rain strove upwards from earth to sky to bear their fruit. But apart from the poetic interpretation of fact there are again very deep psychological matters involved. This kind of myth occurs in dramatic dreams, especially as people begin to face the imminent problem of new sex life flowering within them.

In the village among the corn plantations there lived the most beautiful

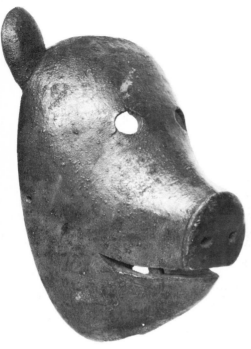

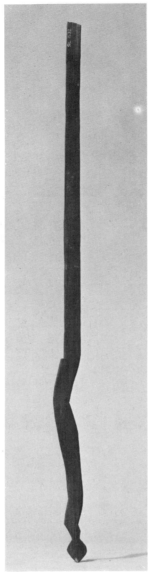

Above. Iroquois masks were designed to emphasise their symbolic importance, not their beauty. This mask reflects the importance of the pig as a food–animal to the Iroquois, just as the corn-husk mask reflects the importance of agriculture. Museum of the American Indian, Heye Foundation, New York.

Right. Swallow-stick used to cause vomiting during cleansing ceremonies. British Museum.

Far right. A wooden False Face mask. These grotesque masks were worn in Iroquois ceremonies in the ritual intended to counteract the influence of the malignant False Face spirits. Although usually horrific in appearance, so as to drive away the evil spirits, some of the masks have a more humourous aspect. New York State Museum, Albany.

Opposite. Heng, the Thunder spirit, Thunder in the atmosphere meant the approach of spring, so Heng was regarded as a kindly spirit and given offerings at the seasonal festivals. Watercolour by Ernest Smith. Rochester Museum of Arts and Sciences, New York.

of all young women. She had been so lost in admiration of her own personality that she found no man fit to marry her. But it happened one day that a most handsome young man arrived beside her. As they looked at each other she fell in love, presently promising to marry him. So he called her to follow him, and she cast aside her past habits and walked after him as a good wife should.

They walked a long way, though it seemed almost no distance. At length they reached his long bark wigwam where she was welcomed by his mother and three sisters. Each day the young man would go out to bring in deer meat while the women worked the fields and prepared skins for clothing. One day however he

returned very tired. His magic was exhausted. He laid his head in his wife's lap and asked her to clean his hair. As she smoothed the long tresses she felt a terrible change. He had returned to his proper shape and became a gigantic serpent. Her mother-in-law then confessed that they were the Serpent People and told her to run away as fast as she could.

The poor girl, sufficiently punished for her earlier pride, was allowed to escape under the protection of Thunder. Once again her long journey seemed short. She could hear a terrible rustling behind her as the serpent followed, but she crossed the mountains and came to a lake near her home. There stood three handsome men. The tallest cast a shining spear at the serpent and pierced it. At once a roaring black cloud enveloped them all, for the great spearman was Thunder himself.

After this the young men escorted the girl to their father's home on the island, where she married the third son. Eventually they had a baby boy who also had thunder power and when he was four years old his toy arrows would knock down trees.

As the boy was so strong and healthy his mother begged to be allowed to visit her own mother on the earth below. Thunder warned her that if she took the child to show her mother she must never let him shoot at people, even in play. For if he made lightning on earth he must return to the sky at once.

At first all went well. The Thunder Boy played peacefully with his companions, but after a while they began to jeer at him because he never went hunting with bow and arrows. Unable to resist their taunts he seized his bow. He shot an arrow towards the boys. Happily the shot went wide and only set some trees on fire. But his grandfather Thunder swept down in his roaring black cloud and carried the boy away to live high in the sky where he was unable to strike men.

As with all hunting peoples the woodland Indians felt the relationship between man and animals to be close. Even their agricultural activities had not exempted them from hunting as their primary source of food. So there were many animals with whom a special relationship had to be established. Some creatures had ceremonial importance, for instance the eagles which flew highest of all birds and hunted animal prey too. Eagle feathers were a brave ornament to be worn by a chief.

The hunter and the eagle

There is a tale of a hunter who was exceptionally successful in hunting deer. He had a magical power of calling them to eat in the pastures near him where they offered an easy target to his arrows. He was not content with this however. He would call to the eagles, saying that here was fresh meat to take to their eyries. The

eagles would descend to eat the meat and then he would shoot them and take their feathers. Everyone warned him that this was dangerous and would bring retribution; but he ignored their warnings.

One day when he called the eagles the gigantic Mother of all Eagles swooped down on him. He fled to hide himself in a hollow log. But Eagle Mother seized the log and carried him to her eyrie. Luckily, he still had his leather carrying-thongs and a little dried meat with him. As the eagle left her nest to seek more food, he fed a little of the meat to each eaglet in turn, and then tied up their beaks with his carrying-thong. For two days the Eagle Mother tried unsuccessfully to release her fledglings. Finally she came to an agreement with the hunter. If he would promise to shoot only deer and never to kill an eagle without the permission of the Spirit World, she would return him to earth safely, provided that he first unbound the beaks of her young. The hunter agreed to do so.

Later, his descendants kept his promise for him. Whenever a deer was killed the shaman called the eagles to come and eat in safety.

The myths of the woodland Indians reflect the new and more intimate relationship between men and the world of nature which men experienced when they began to practise agriculture. The struggle to grow crops in the face of difficulties of land, climate and disease is reflected in myths, such as the story of Tsentsa and Taweskare, which describes a struggle between light and dark, good and misfortune. The more complicated social organisation, which developed in the large, settled, agricultural communities, is reflected in the increased complexity of the subject matter of the myths, such as the elaborate creation myth about the Woman Fallen from the Sky, and the relationship they believed to exist between men and the powers of nature is illustrated by the story of the proud young girl rescued from the serpent by Thunder.

The Buffalo Hunters of the Plains

In prehistoric times the Great Plains of North America were an almost unbroken expanse of grass. The lowland stretched for 1,000 miles (1,600 kilometres) with only occasional hilly ridges. It was intersected by deep-cut river valleys that were often bordered by bluffs. Along these valleys, Indian families settled and grouped themselves into large tribes.

There were a great many Plains tribes, with different languages and customs. Every tribe was composed of several related bands, each numbering a hundred or more people and governed by a chief, who was aided by a council of elders.

Tribal life

When they were first discovered by Europeans, the Plains Indians were practising agriculture as much as hunting. They cultivated maize, several varieties of beans and squash and, like the Iroquois, they had fruit plantations. For part of the year they hunted the buffalo and at other times deer.

Hunting was the work of men. They would drive small groups from the buffalo herds over bluffs, or trap stragglers in pitfalls. Often they erected stockaded corrals into which they would drive buffalo from the rear of the herd.

The pattern of life for these prairie tribes varied with the alternation of summer and winter. In the summer, they lived in tipis, or skin tents, on the wide prairie grasslands. In winter they returned to large earth houses near the rivers and their garden plantations. The earth houses were large constructions with tree trunks erected as pillars to support a small square frame, which was left open as a smoke vent. Encircling the pillars was a low palisade of stakes and brushwood, sunk a few feet below ground, and forming the walls of a sunken room perhaps twenty or thirty feet (six to nine metres) across. From these low walls, poles were arranged sloping up to the central framework. Seen from outside, the whole house looked like a low conical mound with an entrance at one side and a smoke hole on top to allow smoke to escape from the central fireplace below.

Their clothing was simple, all of it made and decorated by the women, and consisting of skin leggings and a shirt for the men and a loose shift or skirt for the women.

During the 18th century, the use of horses, first obtained from Spanish settlements in the southwest, spread throughout the Plains area. With horses, nomadic hunters, such as the Dakota, were able to depend on the buffalo for most of their needs. Some of the farming tribes in the eastern Plains, like the Mandan and Pawnee, now left their settled villages for part of the year to ride after the buffalo; others, like the Cheyenne and Crow, moved westwards and abandoned farming altogether.

The Buffalo Spirits

The buffalo herds, millions of animals strong, moved north and south according to season in immense

The men of the Plains tribes had various societies, pledged to perform particular duties and to fulfil ceremonial functions. This is 'Pehriska-rupa, Moennitarri warrior in the costume of the dog dance'. The costumes, as shown in this 1834 painting by Carl Bodmer, emphasised their war-like character.

When the first Europeans saw the great plains of North America, the buffalo numbered untold millions. The lives and culture of the Plains Indians were closely linked to these great beasts. Then, in a short space of time, white hunters and settlers slaughtered the buffalo, which soon, unbelievably, verged on extinction.

migrations, sweeping through everything in their path. The buffalo was the essential element in Plains Indian culture. Its flesh provided food and its hide material for clothing and shelter. Tools were made from its bones and horns, and thread and string from its sinews. The social life and daily routine of the Plains tribes centred on the buffalo. Naturally, many of their legends related to Buffalo Spirits and to the Earth Mother who gave shelter to the archetypal spirits of buffalo in her underworld home. In times of famine the Indians would pray to her to release more souls to inhabit the bodies of buffaloes and so bring food to the hungry people.

The great festivals
During the summer the tribes tended to break up, family groups separating in order to enjoy easier hunting. A small group could cut off a section of a migrating buffalo herd more easily than a whole tribe of people working together. In the great tribal gatherings at the spring and autumn festivals, the families all came together again. Offerings were made to the spirits of sky and earth and to the tribal ancestors.

Most men belonged to the various ritual societies, such as the 'Dogs', the 'Bulls', the 'Stone Hammers' or the 'Kit-foxes'. The members of these societies were comrades, often of the same age-group, pledged to uphold one another's interests. The societies also had public duties to perform, such as maintaining law and order in the camp, protecting the camp against enemy attack, and organising war parties or communal hunts. At the great festivals the societies performed their sacred rituals, elaborately painted and costumed, and parading before the whole camp.

In times of rest and peace, there were mass sports and games of dexterity. Shinny, a game not unlike hockey, was extremely popular, mostly as a women's sport, and played with teams of hundreds a side. Men played the hoop-and-pole game in which the players rolled a hoop, either netted or plain, and threw darts at it, the manner of striking determining the score.

A world of spirits
The religious beliefs of the Plains Indians centred on an ill-defined, but omnipresent supernatural power which manifested itself all around them – in the sun, moon and stars, in animals and birds, and in natural forces such as wind, thunder and rain. Some tribes developed sophisticated

philosophies concerning the roles of these beings in the universe, but for others they remained mysterious forces which controlled the natural world, but which could be persuaded, through prayers and offerings, to use their powers for the benefit of human beings.

Powerful beings communicated with people through dreams and visions and thus the individual vision quest was an important way of gaining spiritual power. To this end, young men (and sometimes women) would go alone to some desolate place to fast and pray for guidance from the spirits. As a result of their deprivations, they quite often did have visions in which spirits appeared to aid them and to instruct them in the sacred rituals necessary for their success in life.

Similarly, religious festivals, such as the Sun Dance, were occasions for the seeking of powerful visions. The self-mutilation which sometimes occurred during these ceremonies was a means of reinforcing the suppliant's prayers for guidance and of attracting the attention of a spirit who might be moved by pity into granting the power requested.

Nesaru and the creation of the world
The Arikara, a typical people of the prairies, believed man came from a previous world under the earth. The first part of their creation myth recalls that of the woodland Indians about the Woman Fallen from the Sky. The great sky spirit Nesaru (known as Wakonda in the Dakota myths) had charge over the whole of creation. Below his sky world there was a limitless lake where two ducks swam eternally at peace. Suddenly they saw

Wolf-Man and Lucky-Man. These two both asked the ducks to dive and bring up mud to make the earth. Wolf-Man made a great prairie for the animals to live in. But Lucky-Man made undulating ground with hills and valleys where in the future the Indians could hunt and shelter. Between the two regions the great river began to run as it still does.

Then Wolf-Man and Lucky-Man went under the earth to find the Two Spiders. These were male and female beings, dirty and ugly. The two visitors were very surprised to find that these creatures had no knowledge of how to reproduce their species. The visitors set to work to scrub the Two Spiders. They explained to them the wonderful power of fertilisation. Thus enlightened, the Two Spiders began to give birth to all kinds of animals and to a race of giants.

Nesaru was displeased with these giants, who lived under the earth and would not give obedience to him as the Power Above. So he created maize, and sent down its seeds for the animals to take under the earth. The seeds turned into a smaller race of people, like ourselves. Nesaru then sent a flood which destroyed all the giants without harming the new people who were still under the earth. They developed in their dark underworld, began to wonder if there was a better place, and cried for help. Thereupon Nesaru decided that they should come out into the open world. He sent down a woman from his cornfields, the Corn Mother. She walked far and long, but found no one. Then in the east she heard Thunder, who thrust her down into the underworld.

The people and animals clustered around her in the dark underworld. She called upon the gods and the spirits. The animals were inspired to help her. Badger began the work of digging towards the light but could not bear it as he came near the surface. Then Mole dug further, but the first rays of light blinded him, so he remained in his underground burrows. Lastly, Mouse made the breakthrough but the light was so strong that it cut off the long snout

Above A buffalo-hide drum with a painted design illustrating the four quarters into which the world was divided. The Pawnee had an elaborate mythology about the sky, in which the heavens were divided into four quarters and the Morning Star and the Evening Star were great powers. Museum of the American Indian, Heye Foundation, New York.

Opposite Chief Mató-tope. A Mandan chief drawn by Carl Bodmer in 1834 and printed in Maximilian *Travels*, 1843. The eagle-feather headdress is a symbol of chieftainship. The feathered spear and the horns show that he is a medicine man as well.

which he once had and he became a short-nosed mouse. Then Corn Mother began to thrust her way into the light. Earth was still tight and close around her. Then Thunder roared again in the east and shook the earth loose so that Corn Mother and the whole creation of humans and animals could come up to the surface.

The people followed the trail westwards from the place of emergence. Many adventures followed. Kingfisher pointed the way, Owl led them through the dark forest, and Loon led them across the lake.

They were given maize to plant, and taught how to play games like shinny. Corn Mother returned to the sky. Left to themselves, the people began to quarrel and fight about the games. Many were killed. But one day they saw beside the lake a wonderful man dressed as a chief. His hair was beautiful and hung down to his waist. He carried a staff hung with captured scalps. It was Nesaru, and he told them how to live at peace together and work under the leadership of a chief. He showed them how to conduct wars, and gave them the rules of honour which included the taking of scalps. These scalps were to be marks of bravery and show which of the warriors was best suited to become a war chief. Then Corn Mother stood beside him to teach them how to grow maize. She told them of the stars, planets, sun and moon and the gods in the sky. Lastly she told them that they must take the sacred symbols which would be given to them, and wrap them up so they would become the sacred medicine-bundles which would help them through all dangers.

The people made offerings to the Gods of the Eight Directions of the Sky. Then there was a roaring sound. It was the Wind of the Southeast who had been forgotten. He was like a tornado, and everyone he touched fell dead from disease. But a dog was sent from the sun with medicine to cure them. It told the people about the diseases of man and how to cure them, and explained the reason for the turbulent anger of the Wind of

the Southeast. Then the people made the offerings necessary to appease him and learned to cure diseases. Because of this, whenever the Arikara held a ceremony, they sacrificed a dog so that its spirit would go to take messages to the gods.

Nesaru and Corn Mother left the people, warning them that offerings of tobacco smoke must be offered regularly to the Gods of the Eight Directions. Nesaru left his medicine-bundle among them and Corn Mother gave them a great cedar tree to represent her.

The medicine-bundle
Among all the Indian tribes, but particularly those of the Great Plains, the concept of the medicine-bundle was central to the practice of religion. There were few sacred buildings of any kind. Those there were included open constructions such as the Sun-Dance Lodge, where people offered their ceremonies to the spirits above and where men would make offerings of their physical suffering because the Indians associated physical and spiritual expression as complementary to the whole. Some of the sacred places were those where great happenings had occurred.

One of the most famous was the 'Sacred Canoe' of the Mandans, which was made of ancient willow boards believed to come from a palisade in which the first ancestors had been rescued from the primeval flood. Instead of sacred places the Indians venerated the medicine-bundles, which were in effect portable shrines. The Indians believed that they contained relics of the first ancestors, or sacred objects given by the gods to protect man and bring good fortune. In this they were almost identical to the sacred bundles preserved among the highly civilised Aztecs of Mexico, and similar to the sacred bundles, called *tjurungas*, kept by the Australian Aborigines and the sacred objects, such as the Palladia, which were preserved in the holy places of classical Europe.

The medicine-bundle, however, was regarded as a form of property. It could change hands, though often

bundle was brought into the teepee. A pole with offerings and gifts for the gods was set up in front of it, and the people were warned that they must sit in complete silence. The priests sang many chants and struck the pole three times, and then four times, invoking the Buffalo Spirits. They reminded the buffalo that they had promised to come when the people who were in want performed the ceremony before the buffalo medicine-bundle.

After three days they heard the thunder of the advancing herds. Then the priests sent out some chosen young men to capture a young bull and bring it entire to the chief's lodge. The young men did this, bringing a complete carcass, unmarked save for a single lance thrust. It was laid on the floor of the big tipi while the priests recited the myth of the Buffaloes Who Became People. Thus would the buffalo medicine-bundle be strengthened in its power to protect the people and bring the animals to feed the tribe.

There was once a village of the Buffalo, who in those days resembled strong human beings wearing horns. In the Buffalo village they kept the sacred bundle called 'Knot in the Tree'. After singing magic chants for four days, the Buffalo priests went to an ancient cottonwood tree and struck a knot in its trunk three times and four times. Then they heard a sound like people crying and talking under the ground. Soon a great many people came up out of the tree. Cut-Nose was the first man out. The Buffalo people hunted them like animals. Cut-Nose ran fast but many others were clubbed and cut up for a great feast of human flesh. Cut-Nose circled and sped back to the tree avoiding the clubs thrown at him. He leapt inside and warned other people against coming out. The flesh of the human victims was then cut up and the Buffaloes danced as the meat was put on drying frames.

One human escaped. He was a young man who was a very fine runner. He was chased by a white Buffalo woman but he outdistanced her. He hid among the grape vines and tangled bushes of a ravine.

only within the family to whose ancestor it had first been entrusted. High values in skins and food had to be exchanged in return for a bundle – similar in a way to the medieval practice of bartering the relics of saints between one cathedral and another. The medicine-bundle rights included the songs, dances, and ritual costumes connected with it. The sacred object was the focus of an entire myth, almost a materialisation of an archetype. Its properties are illustrated in the following myth from the Arikara people.

The Knot in the Tree

There was a time when the autumn buffalo hunt had failed. All the people went unfed. The children cried with hunger. The women begged the chief to call on the keepers of the 'Knot in the Tree' medicine-bundle to call for help. So the chief took sacred tobacco, offered its smoke to the gods and asked the priests to open the sacred bundle to make the buffalo come. The priests who guarded the bundle first made the chief clean his tipi and purify the ground inside.

When all was ready the sacred

This young man found small animals to eat as well as berries. He moved from one sheltered place to another. One day he saw a beautiful horned woman dressed in white leather. Her hair hung below her waist. The young man followed her. He saw her go into a fine painted tipi. He followed. She bade him welcome and invited him to sleep with her. So they lay in each others' arms, covered by her robe of white skin. As he looked hungry she gave him some meat. Then he slept. When he awoke there was no tipi at all.

Buffalo-Girl told how the Buffalo people wanted to be turned into true animals, but that the man who could work the magic was not to be found. She had selected him to be the hero. But he must brave the danger of the angry flesh-eating Buffalo men if he was to win. He must get to the chief's tipi through four rows of guards. She covered him in a buffalo skin and led him as far as the guardian warriors. Some thought they could smell human meat, but others told them

that was because they had all became spotted with human blood during the hunt. At last the young man came to the chief's tipi. Buffalo-Girl led him to where he could rest in a pile of animal skins.

He overheard the chief reciting the hunting chants and learned the way to use the ash staff to strike the magic tree when calling the food people. He dared not sleep for fear of betraying himself. In the morning when the chief went out to lead another great hunt, Buffalo-Girl came in and to give him courage, showed him the high racks on which meat was drying. He climbed up and saw human ribs, hands, breasts, and some heads. His anger gave him strength.

Buffalo-Girl next took him to a copse near the sacred tree. There she told him to cut ash staves and trim them into bows. He must take straight twigs and canes to make arrows. He must use strips of skin to make bow strings. For a long time he worked and made as many as he could, ready for the fight. Then

Buffalo-Girl went with him to the tree. She called through it to Cut-Nose and told him that when the time came he must take the bow and arrow offered to him and shoot a Buffalo man. Everyone with him was to do the same.

Next day they carried the bows to the tree and hid them under a buffalo-skin.

The chief came with his warriors. He chanted while he struck the tree three times and then four times. There was a sound of voices, and Cut-Nose emerged. He took his bow and ran quickly beyond the Buffalo men. Then the other people came up and each took a bow. As they did so they shot at the Buffalo men, who were so frightened that they fled. Each took with him a piece of the stored human flesh, which he tucked under his armpit. None gave fight, but as each one was hit he turned into a real buffalo and grazed on the prairie grass instead of eating humans.

Buffalo-Girl married the young man, and their children founded the

Arikara nation. Now, whenever the 'Knot in the Tree' medicine-bundle is opened, the ceremonies and dances are those which Buffalo-Girl taught the first Arikara. And whenever the Arikara hunt buffalo for food, they leave uneaten the lump under the buffalo's foreleg; it is believed that this is human meat from their ancestors.

The Okipa ceremony

Among the Mandan the great annual ceremony was known as the Okipa. Dances lasted many days: great men offered their pain in exchange for the good of the world: and the sacred legends of the beginnings of things were recounted by the elders among the priests. The story of creation was owned by 'The Lone Man' medicine-bundle.

Lone Man

Lone Man was walking on the great waters. He did not know how he had come into being. He turned back and followed his tracks and found a blood-striped flower. The red flower spoke, saying that she had given birth to him so that he might go about in the world. He knew there must be something below the waters from which his mother had her life. He saw two ducks and commanded them to bring earth up from below the waters. They brought up four pieces which Lone Man scattered. The pieces formed four directions, and bore grass and fruit trees.

Lone Man went to many places, and everywhere new things came into being. After many adventures he came across Coyote, who called himself First Man. They quarrelled about their names and about who was the elder. Lone Man speared First Man, who died. Lone Man waited a time and saw that First Man had become a skeleton and the spear was broken. He was pleased that he had proved he was the elder. But as he moved his spear, the bones clicked together again and First Man Coyote stood alive once more before him. So they decided to hunt together. They made different kinds of country, and filled them all with animals. Then they discovered that the Indians were living on the land.

Lone Man wanted to be one with the Indians so he looked around to find a woman who would take him inside her body so that he could be born. He saw a girl chewing maize, but thought she might break him up before he got inside. Then he saw another very beautiful woman, who was fishing with her mother. He became a dead buffalo floating in the stream, with some kidney fat showing through a wound in his back. The girl snatched the tasty fat and swallowed it. She suddenly felt strange and called her mother. She became big with child and gave birth to a fine boy with magical black marks on his forehead.

The child grew with unprecedented speed. Soon he was a young man. He desired beautiful clothes. Spotted Eagle Hoita lived nearby. He had a fine white buckskin coat. The young Lone Man called Wind and it blew the coat far away. The Rain and Sun made the coat more beautiful than ever. It was found by some travelling Indians, who said it was far finer than the coat worn by Hoita. They brought it with them to the village and gave it to Lone Man. This offended Hoita, who went off in a huff and took all the animals with him to the Dog Den and kept them there. Lone Man sometimes saw animals pass by to the north. He was disturbed about the migration. He met Mouse-Woman who warned him that his property was being turned into animals which all became white and went northwards. On her advice he turned himself into a white hare. He came to the Dog Den, and managed to hide safely.

Hoita led the animals in a magic dance and sang a chant that would make a famine in Lone Man's village. The power of the dance came from the beating of the drum made from a great roll of hide. Once Lone Man had learned this he slipped away in search of a more powerful medicine-drum. He called all the creatures but none could help except the Giant Turtles who supported the earth in the waters. As they could not move without destroying the earth Lone Man made a copy of their form, stretching leather over it to make a drum and decorating the neck with feathers. He made the frame of oak, because it was oak-wood which held the earth on the back of the Giant Turtles.

When Lone Man played on his new medicine-drum Hoita was perplexed. He sent the animals to find out what it was, but one by one Lone Man trapped them and gave them to his people. Hoita then realised he was defeated and released the remaining animals from Dog Den, telling them to scatter, so that wherever the Mandan people travelled they should find the food which they asked for.

Lone Man was persecuted by a being known as Maninga; but by trickery and cunning he defeated him. Maninga retreated but four years later returned for a last test of strength. He came as a great flood. At this time there were five Mandan villages full of people, and as the flood came higher the villages were abandoned one by one. Lone Man led his people up to the last village. There he planted a sacred cedar tree to represent himself and the people. Then he built a small stockade of willow planks. It was called the Great Canoe, though it never floated. As the flood grew, it lapped the sides of the Great Canoe. Maninga drew clear in order to destroy the Mandans. But Lone Man knew that he was fond of shell ornaments and threw the most precious shells over the stockade wall. Maninga let the flood recede so that he could pick them up. Then the magic of the turtle-drum was made and Maninga was swept away with the receding waters. The cedar tree stood for many centuries, and some of the stockade that the Indians believed to be the remains of the Great Canoe, can still be seen at the old Mandan village on the left bank of the Upper Missouri.

After many victories over the hostile powers of nature, Lone Man departed to the southwest, leaving the Mandans with the cedar tree memorial, and the great medicine-bundles used in the Okipa Ceremony.

The Nuptadi Robe
The story of the medicine-bundle known as 'Nuptadi (Young Grandmother) Robe' sheds some light on early Indian custom, for the robe itself is a very old and small garment like an apron, not worn by any tribe in historic times, and the tale begins with clear evidence that it dates from the days before the arrival of the horse.

The early Indians harnessed dogs to drag a travois of trailing wooden poles to carry their possessions when they moved camp. One day as a boy was sitting on a travois First Man Coyote, who made the earth, ran by. The dog, seeing a coyote, chased it, dragging travois and boy with him. Lost and far from his village, the boy found a bow and some arrows and thanked the spirit who had left them. Then he saw a buffalo bull, shot at it, and felled it although he did not pierce its hide. He sought a sharp stone and cut open the back of the bull to extract the rich kidney fat. Then, as he needed something hard to make tools, he took a leg bone from the bull and struck it against a stone until it broke. A splinter flew off and where it fell he found a baby girl.

The boy had proved himself. Coyote reappeared in human form. He told the boy to bring some sage. Then he set it on fire. He passed the baby girl through the smoke four times. Each time she grew older. When the last smoking was over the girl was big enough to cook and make fine buffalo robes, and the boy had become a young man. Coyote was satisfied that they could now support each other, and left them.

They both worked well and built themselves a sound tipi to live in. One day the girl asked her foster-brother if he should not find himself a wife, for there were some girls approaching and by the time they had built them-

selves their winter earth-house the girls would come.

Sure enough, two beautiful girls arrived, and the boy asked them if they would stay as his wives. They agreed, although they warned him that his foster-sister had complained of his violent temper.

Soon after their arrival the wives warned the young man that his foster-sister needed an extra human scalp to ornament a new robe that she was making. Curious, he looked at the bundle containing the robe when she was out, burning sweet grass and praying that he would not be overcome by magic as he did so. He saw that it was a shell robe, with a man's scalp under each of the clam shells

sewn on it. An empty space on the shoulder clearly awaited another scalp. Then he recalled that she cooked and ate her meat secretly. Now he guessed that she was a supernatural creature who ate human flesh. When his foster-sister came back, she passed the bundle containing her new robe and then touched her foster-brother's garments. As she did so they gave off a flash of blue fire. He also had supernatural powers. He ran to the white skin tipi of his wives, and in the ensuing combat managed to shoot his foster-sister who told him that her time on earth had come to an end. Now he must take her magic shell robe and preserve it, so that her powers might benefit the Mandans.

As she died he took the robe and made the magical Nuptadi Robe bundle with it.

The Pawnee

Well to the south of the Great Plains lived the Pawnee. They moved gradually northwards, planting and hunting until, when the white men met them, they were hunting around the Platte River. They spoke one of the Caddoan languages spoken by their remote ancestors. They were a confederation of smaller tribes who shared a common culture. The name Pawnee, derived from a word meaning 'a horn', was adopted because their young men used to gather up their hair and coil it back

In Pawnee mythology the bodies of two star rulers were placed on burial frames in the sky. This reflects the Indian custom of placing the bodies of their dead on frames near the village. The body was painted and oiled, dressed in its best robes and supplied with arms and provisions. A buffalo skin from a freshly killed animal was tightly bound around the body. Other robes were soaked in water to soften them, then bandaged round the body and tied fast so as to exclude the action of air. Later, when the flesh had quite dried away, the bones were buried in rock crevices. This is a funeral scaffold of a Sioux chief, painted by Carl Bodmer, 1934.

over their foreheads as a queue or pigtail bound with hide and stiffened with grease. The Pawnee were famed for their courage and intelligence. They put up a brave resistance to the white invaders but eventually abandoned the old customs and adopted new ways.

The ancient Pawnee tribes were especially interested in the gods of the sky. There were among them astronomers who watched the movements of the planets and decided the most propitious times for making offerings. They particularly venerated the North Star as a beneficent creator god, and went in fear of the magical South Star, who was a force of opposition belonging to the underworld. Morning Star, who led the sun up into the sky, was their protector. Evening Star, who drove the sun down to the darkness, was a dangerous enemy spirit who sent his daughter to hinder the creative powers of the Morning Star, although eventually, when she had been pierced by magic arrows and lay dying, she gave great blessings.

The Morning Star myth

One of the more important bundles was the 'Morning Star' bundle. The story connected with this bundle consisted of two halves, one telling the myth of Morning Star and the Evening Star Girl. Its ritual climax occurred in four-yearly cycles. The young warriors had to creep up to an enemy camp and capture a young woman. She was kept a while and treated kindly so that she could carry good messages to the gods. Then, on the appointed day, she was stripped naked and painted half red and half black to symbolise the Morning and Evening Stars. Then she was tied to a scaffold and the young warriors killed her with a shower of arrows. Her blood was believed to revive a blessing given for the people long ago and to ensure better fortune over the following four years.

The Moon Basket

The other part of the sacred bundle enshrined a stellar myth connected with the Moon Basket.

Above Contents of a Crow male rock medicine bundle. Montana. Museum of the American Indian, Heye Foundation, New York.

When the world was created, the gods decided to make the First People. Two mud figures were made, one of a girl and one of a boy. The boy was given a bow and arrows so that he might hunt for food. Then, while the earth was still in darkness the gods made all the animals pass in front of the boy. He was to shoot one, and whichever he shot would determine the conditions they would create for him. The boy hesitated, fearing to shoot an 'unfavourable' animal, and waited until the last creature came by. His arrow sped true, for he had magical strength and a black and white buffalo cow fell in its tracks. The condition determined by his choice was the alternation of light and darkness, of day and night.

The young man and woman hunted in the forest, and built themselves grass huts as they needed shelter. One evening they heard a distant drumming that lasted all night. They followed the sound and soon

Opposite 'Little Wound', an Oglala Dakota chief, *c*. 1900.

87

distinguished voices singing sacred chants. In a forest glade they came upon a small plantation of maize and a well constructed lodge where a festival was in progress. As they approached, a woman asked them into the lodge. They entered and in the dim light they saw the central altar where four old men, painted with red earth mixed with grease, chanted and beat the medicine-drums for the dance to begin. The dancers were a great crowd of girls. This was the house of Moon Lady and her daughters the stars.

The round dance began. The First People were told to watch so that they would understand the dance of the stars.

The old men who led the chant were Wind, Cloud, Lightning, and Thunder, the four powers of the sky. During the dance the Evening Star Woman stood in front of the altar, slightly to the west. In the sacred basket she held the Moon. In front of her to the east, there danced four other women, who were the daughters of Big Black Meteor Star (possibly Algol or Capella) who stands to the north-east in the sky of the Pawnees. Big Black Meteor Star was the star of magic, who would later be the instructress of the medicine men. His daughters danced to the west, each carrying a basket in which there were two white skins of swan's necks and two white fawn skins. They laid their baskets with the symbols at the feet of Evening Star Woman and the dance ended.

The basket was a magic one. When the Indians made copies for the dance on earth, they were not allowed to use a knife but had to break the withies by hand, and when it was woven they lined it with mud and water. This symbolised creation. The swan's neck skins and the fawn skins represented the two pairs of gods who stood in the west, the region of Evening Star Woman.

The First People were given the basket they had learned to make, together with twelve sticks and many plumstones. This would remind them that Tirawa Atius the Power Above, made Moon (who was mother of the

stars) and the twelve great stars (probably the Pleiades). The sticks and the plumstones were to be thrown down in a gambling game so that people should play and understand the mysteries of the movement of the stars through the apparent falling of chance.

This was the story of the medicine-bundle that contained the Moon Basket. In places where neither houses nor lights obscure the night sky one can understand a little of the reverence with which the Pawnee, like all ancient peoples, regarded the stars. The heavens showed the continuation of regular movement in the dance of life; the sudden changes of fate were shown in shooting stars. They believed that one day they would see in the sky the signs which would mean the end of the world. The Pawnee thought that the Pole Stars, North and South, would move together when the end came.

The end of the world

In earlier times the Pawnee believed that the world would end in a different way. The elders sang about Tirawa Atius the Power Above. They chanted to the beat of the drums; they rattled their gourds as they sang before the medicine-bundle. There was a time when Tirawa Atius had placed giant people on the earth. But the giants grew proud and had to be destroyed. Storms came from the northwest; the waters rose and rain poured down. The race of giants was destroyed; the last of them were supposed to have died on a hill in Kansas. (The bones discovered there, on which the Indians based their myth, have been shown by modern science to be dinosaur bones.)

Human beings were made. In the northwest Tirawa Atius set a great buffalo bull to hold that corner of the sky. Each year the bull lost a single hair. When all the hairs had fallen out the world would come to an end for the present human race.

Tirawa Atius had placed the gods in the sky: the groups of four deities for each quarter of the heavens, the moving stars, the Sun and Moon. He would consult with them all if he had

to threaten humans with destruction. Morning Star was appointed to rule over the lesser gods, and together with Evening Star had power of giving life to the people on earth. Sun and Moon also gave life but they were not great powers like Morning Star.

The Pawnee believed that when the end was coming they would be warned by the moon changing to a dark colour and then to black. On the day that the cataclysm was to take place the sun would become dim quite quickly and then suddenly all would be dark, darker than in an eclipse, and that darkness without light would be the end for the human race. Sometimes the South Star was given permission to move through the heavens to look on the North Star so that it could rest assured that North Star was in the right position. Then it would move back and the stars resume their dance.

And in the heavens there were warnings of death too. At the first great council of the gods two of the star rulers died, one old and one young. Their bodies were wrapped and placed on frames, just as the Indians wrapped their dead and placed them on high racks so that their bones should be nearer the stars. There were two burial frames in the sky which always moved around the

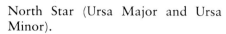
North Star (Ursa Major and Ursa Minor).

The North Star was aware of fate and warned the people that when the South Star moved through the heavens it came a little further north each time. One day it would swing high enough to capture the People on the Frames. On that night the ruler of the earth and its people would change and the South Star would then resume dominion.

As the end came nearer there would be meteor showers, and the sun would change colour like a rainbow before the final darkness. The final commands for the destruction would come from the west and be obeyed in the east. The skies would move. The North Star would command and the South Star carry out the work. The stars would come to earth and the Indians would become stars too and live in the place ruled by the South Star, which is their true home.

The important role played by the sun, moon and stars in Pawnee mythology grows out of their experience of the movement of the stars across the vast sky of the prairies. In the regular patterns of the stars in the night sky the Indians saw a symbol of the pattern of life and expressed this in veneration of the Sky Father. The Mandan myths are exceptional

among the myths of the Buffalo hunters in that they deal with more complicated subjects, such as the story of Lone Man and the universal theme of creation, and tell them in a more vivid and elaborate style.

The spread of agriculture among the Plains tribes is reflected in the myths about Corn Mother and the coming of maize, but the major preoccupation of the Plains Indians, the hunting of the great buffalo herds, is illustrated in what is probably the most typical of their myths, the Arikara story of the Buffalo people.

Above. The Crow Sun Dance was held by someone seeking revenge for the murder of a close relation. During the ceremony he was required to stare at the sacred doll until he received the vision of a scalped enemy. Museum of the American Indian, Heye Foundation, New York.

Left, above. A red stone pipe bowl from East Dakota. Smoking was very often a ceremonial activity and pipes were decorated with religious scenes. The carving on this pipe shows a shaman receiving instruction from a bear spirit. Linden-Museum, Stuttgart.

Left, below. Arapaho painted buffalo skull used in ceremonies. Museum of the American Indian, Heye Foundation, New York.

The Hunters of the Southwest

In the far west of North America the Indian tribes were mostly small groups of people living on what they could gather under the semi-desert conditions. On the Pacific coast, around the region which is now Los Angeles, tribes were few and poor, living on shell fish and a few small wild animals. Inland they collected acorns from the local species of oak, crushed them into flour strained through water to remove the tannic acid, and baked the paste on hot stones to make a fine, almost tasteless, wafer bread. These people have their own typical hunting mythologies and ancestor tales, but they are of the simple type already represented in our collection of Inuit stories.

The Navajo

The southwestern area largely comprises the present-day states of Arizona and New Mexico. It is a geographically diverse region. Although much of it is arid scrubland, there are also high mountains clothed with pine and juniper, and broad valleys with small wooded oases around the seasonal streams and washes.

Because of their linguistic affinities with tribes in Canada and Alaska, it is generally believed that the Navajo and the related Apache migrated from the north, ariving in the Southwest about 600 years ago. In pre-Columbian times they led semi-nomadic lives, hunting small game and gathering edible roots, seeds and berries. They also learned some agricultural techniques from the Pueblo peoples already settled in the area, and the extent to which the Navajo adopted agriculture can be deduced from their name, derived from 'Apaches

de Nabaju' – 'Apaches of the cultivated fields' – given to them by 17th-century Spanish explorers to distinguish them from the other Apache groups.

At this period Navajo clothing was of skin, although cotton garments were sometimes traded from the Pueblos. With the introduction of domestic livestock into the area by Spanish settlers, the Navajo became shepherds, building up large flocks of sheep and goats. From the Pueblo Indians they learned to spin and weave the wool provided by their flocks and to make their clothing

from it. They remained semi-nomadic, in summer living in temporary brushwood shelters and in winter moving back to their earth-covered timber huts, called hogans.

The shaman

Shamans were known to all the tribes of the Southwest and were considered to be in close contact with the spirit world of gods and ancestors, and with the spirits of Maize, the Rainbow, the Sun, Thunder and all the powers of nature. A powerful shaman could be expected to advise on future events, to guide people in the proper ritual for curing illness or for protecting crops. He was regarded as a holy man.

His initiation, like that of the shamans of the northern Indians, the Inuit and the Plains tribes, was by selection from the spirit world. A boy of eleven or twelve would follow the usual custom of going out into the wild alone for perhaps three or four days to seek a spirit protector. He would travel far without seeking food, praying for help and protection from the spirit world. At the end of this period he would be favoured with a vision. Sometimes spirits would

Scrubland, typical of some of the southwest, on the present-day Navajo reservation in New Mexico

appear in animal form, sometimes as humans, but bigger and more powerful than men, like the Rainbow Maiden or the Thunder Spirit or the Spirit of Hail. Any of these beings could appear to impress the sensitive youth, and often they would promise to guide and direct him through life. It was possible for young girls also to have such experiences.

Once he had had his vision of his spirit-protector, the young man would return to his village and recount his dreams and visions to his relatives. If his relatives found the visions significant, he would be introduced to the religious societies where he would learn the chants describing the gods and the spirit world, and the proper rituals for healing and for seeking inspiration.

Montezuma

We know a little of the more primitive background of the Navajo from the mythologies of the scattered desert peoples, such as the Papago, whose creation legend makes the typical First Man figure into a dual-natured demiurge (creator of the universe) who was once called First Man, but who later became Montezuma. The name reflects the Aztec influences which were carried northwards by the Spanish invaders.

The story tells how he created a human race, how he helped them and occasionally brought trouble to them, how four attempts were made to kill him, and how four times he came to life again to bring still greater scourges. He even created a huge eagle which destroyed many of the first people. The quarrel between the people and the god became irreconcilable. The time came for a new human race to be released from its home underneath the earth. The new race attacked and destroyed the previous people. Then, after having taught them to hunt and grow maize, Montezuma went away to an underground house farther south.

In this legend the basic myths of many American Indians are present in a very simple form. Whether the behaviour of the Montezuma of Papago mythology reflects the

behaviour of Mexican mercenaries advancing with the Spanish conquerers in the 16th century cannot of course be proved, but it may well be so.

Navajo sand-paintings

Much of Navajo ritual and mythology was borrowed from their Pueblo neighbours, but, as with their material borrowings, they adapted, elaborated and refined the various elements to conform to their own cultural style and thus made them very much their own.

Navajo religion is based on the maintenance of a harmonious relationship between man and the spirit world. Should the balance of this relationship be upset, disasters and catastrophe might ensue, manifested in flood, famine or personal misfortune and sickness. Only through the correct performance of appropriate rituals could harmony be restored and disaster averted or illness cured. In ancient Greece, cycles of plays presenting the myths were a poetic expression of the relationship between gods and men. Similarly, the Navajo expressed this relationship by the performance of a ceremonial called a chant or song, which consisted of a series of symbolic acts, unified by a song sequence and usually incorporating one or more sand-painting. The sand-painting, made during the ceremony and then erased, was an expression of the understanding between the spirits and the shaman, who depicted the spirits in colours made from sand, charcoal, cornmeal and pollen. Through their depiction the spirit's power could be attracted and used for the good of the community or individual. A curing ceremony might last from four to nine days, and the ceremonies were all linked with the appropriate myth.

The Navajo developed a series of lengthy and complex myths which preserved their general form through long periods of entirely oral transmission. Some variation was permitted, since each shaman had inherited variations from his teachers, and indeed each shaman might be inspired to improvise in order to

clarify his story. At the beginning of this century one of these shamans recited his stories into phonograph cylinder records for Miss Mary Wheelwright, who founded the Museum of Navajo Ceremonial Art at Santa Fe. Here, many of the sand-paintings, as well as sound recordings and published accounts of Indian mythology, can be studied, and by such means an almost complete record of Navajo religion has been preserved for our own time.

The emergence myth

The most important of the Navajo myths was the emergence myth, the story of creation. The version which follows dates from 1882 when the Navajo were not greatly influenced by European thought.

The present world is the Fifth World. In the First World there were three beings in the darkness: First Man, First Woman and Coyote (the trickster-creator). The First World was too small for them. They travelled to the Second World, where there were two men who became Sun and Moon and where there was a dim and misty light. In the east was black-

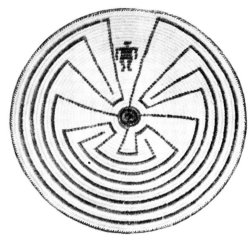

ness, in the south blueness, in the west yellowness and in the north whiteness. Sometimes the blackness would intensify and overshadow all the world, leaving night; soon the colours would glow again, bringing day; each of the four colours concealed a personage who lived within it. When the three beings arrived in the Second World, Sun tried to make love to First Woman and there was discord. Coyote, who knew everything, called the dwellers of north, south, east and west to arbitrate. They decided that the Second World was too small and they should all climb to the Third World where there would be room for Sun to separate from First Woman for ever.

They ascended to the Third World, a wide and beautiful land like the earth. At the corners there were four mountains. At the foot of the mountains there were lakes. And on the slopes of the mountains there were people. The newcomers were met at the Place of Ascent by the mountain people. They were welcomed and warned that all would be well for them so long as Tieholtsodi, the water-monster, was left in peace.

Now Coyote ignored the mountain people's counsel. He was inquisitive and went to look at the great waters. He went to the eastern waters and found two of the children of Tieholtsodi who were so attractive that he took them off to his home wrapped in a blanket. The monster searched the four corners of the world for his children. Unable to find them he guessed that they must be with the new people. The only way he could recover them was by using his power over water. Thereupon the four oceans filled and the water began to rise. All the people held council and determined to escape the flood by removing the mountains of the four directions to pile them one on top of the other in the middle of the land. Still the flood rose. The people planted a giant reed on the top of the piled-up mountain.

When the reed was fully grown it reached the sky and pierced into the Fourth World. The ancestors and the animals they had found in the Third World all climbed inside the reed. Last to come was Turkey who was to sound the alarm when his feet were wet by the flood. When he did so they began to climb up inside the giant reed. On the fourth night they emerged from the top of the reed into

the Fourth World. Even now turkeys have light-coloured tail feathers to show where their ancestor had his tail feathers washed by the flood.

The Fourth World was larger again than the Third. It was dim, lit only by three great mists of light, and obscured from time to time by misty darkness. The mountains and seas were like those of the Third World but in the central plain flowed a great river. On the north bank lived human beings, and on the south other people, who were in animal form. Time passed swiftly in that world. The year resembled a day. But trouble was to follow.

A vicious quarrel developed in which each sex claimed to be the source of sustenance and life. The women argued that they made fire, prepared cotton, planted the fields and made pottery. They also bore the children. The men countered that they hunted and worked hard clearing the fields and building the houses, and – most important – that they knew the ways of the gods and performed the dances and ceremonies needed to make the crops grow. In the end men and women decided to separate. The men made a boat and crossed the river in the central plain, leaving the women to cultivate their

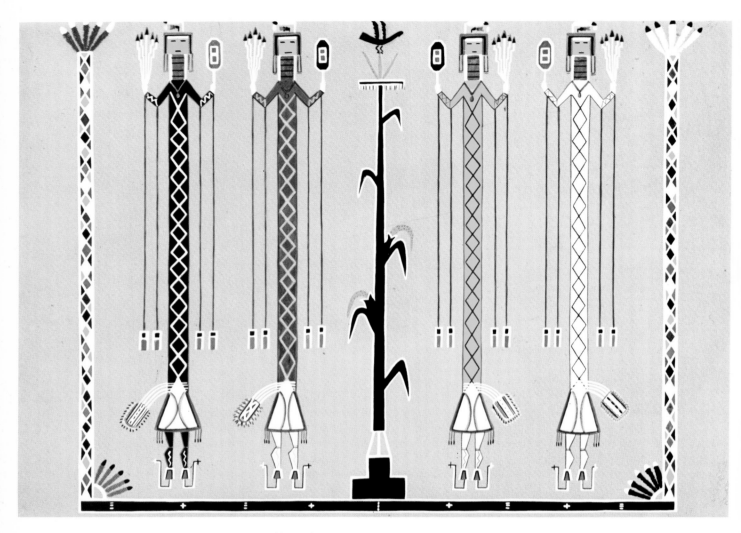

Above. Sand-painting from the Hail Chant, in which the Thunder People, surround a central stalk of black maize topped by a yellow-breasted blackbird. All their masks are made of yellow evening light with white stripes of dawn at the forehead. Museum of Navajo Ceremonial Art, Santa Fé, New Mexico.

Opposite. A sand-painting design reproduced on a textile. The elements included in the design varied, not only according to the Chant which it illustrated, but also to take account of the particular ailment of the patient for whose benefit the Chant was being performed.

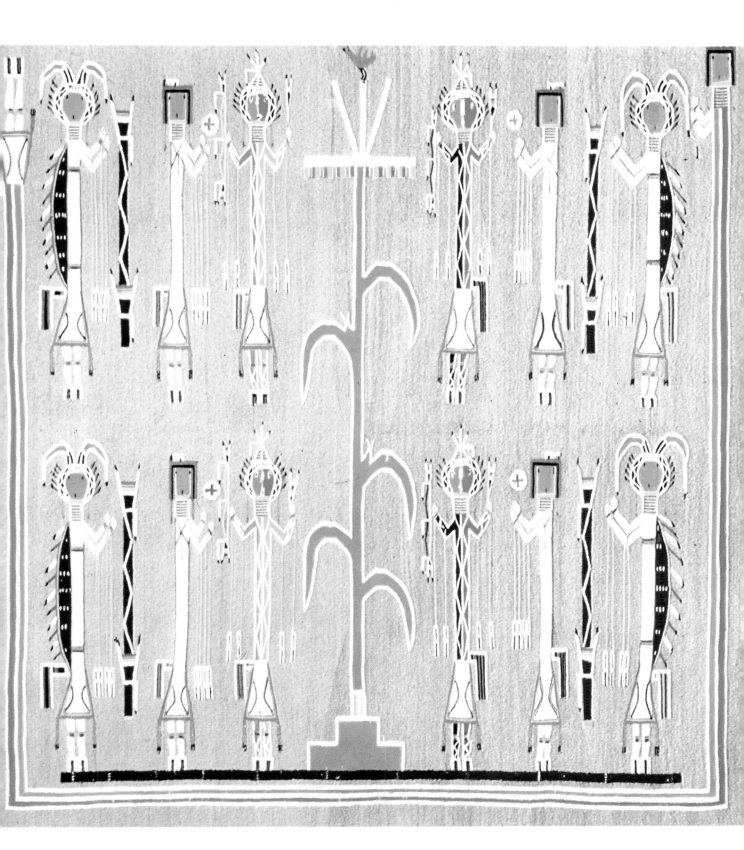

little fields without the propitious dances and ceremonial.

So it continued for four years. The women dug no new ground, and their crops grew less and less. The men dug fresh soil and each year they produced better crops; they also had plenty of reserve food from hunting. But the men were aggrieved that they should have to work so hard tending the fields, while the women were not happy about sowing new ones. They agreed that they were indispensable to each other, and joined forces again.

Having learned this salutary lesson in social discipline, man might have been expected to develop in peace. But Coyote was still among them, still holding the children of the water-monster Tieholtsodi. The world, so recently made more secure by the new understanding between man and women, was threatened by another danger. The ground became soft, the waters burst in, and again the flood menaced the people. Again the mountains of the four directions were piled together in the central plain. Again a great reed was planted and again grew to the earthen sky above the Fourth World.

Badger was the one who went first, digging away the earth above them. But when he found that he was emerging into a muddy lake, there was consternation. No one knew what to do, and the flood was rising. Locust alone felt that he might be able to slip through and find a way. So up he went. He flew to the surface, and there he saw four beautiful swans, who were like the lights of the underworlds, black in the east, blue in the south, yellow in the west and white in the north. The swans questioned Locust and he told them his sad story. But they imposed a magical test before admitting anyone. They demanded that everyone who came up into their world should take an arrow, thrust it into his mouth, pass it right through his body and draw it out of his anus. Then the process had to be reversed and the arrow returned from the mouth. The swans were able to do this without difficulty, but Locust realised that people could not do it. So he agreed, on condition that

the swans in turn would do as he did. He took an arrow, thrust it apparently through the middle of his chest, drew it out at the other side, and then returned it the same way. The swans did not know that Locust was different from other creatures because he had only a narrow spine in the middle of his body, joining the head to the rest, beneath which the arrow could pass safely. They agreed that in view of the phenomenal powers on both sides there need be no further ordeals.

The way was opened and up surged people and animals, hard pressed by the pursuing flood. Each carried a bundle of his most precious possessions. They climbed into the marshy lake, but still the water below surged after them. Suddenly they saw the horns of Tieholtsodi appear in the midst of the land. Overcome with a sense of some hidden guilt, they all came together and showed what was in their packs. Unable to do otherwise, Coyote was forced to reveal the stolen monster-children. His fellows cast them back to their parent. The monsters swam away, and the waters receded to the underworld.

At the Place of Emergence the people found themselves standing on an island in the middle of a swamp. They prayed to the god of darkness in the east, and he cut open the surrounding cliffs with his curved knife. The remaining waters drained away but the swamp was dangerously soft and the people still could not move. Anxiously they prayed to the Four Winds. A gale arose and for four days they waited. Then the earth dried out and hardened, and they reached the shores of the swamp in safety. As the earth was not yet properly formed, they took piles of mud to make the four mountains at its corners. The mountains hardened and grew as the earth expanded. When the boundaries were marked, they took Sun and Moon and threw them up into the sky. At first Sun was too near the earth. On four successive days the earth was expanded and the Sun flew higher. On the fifth day Sun stood still at its zenith. Everything was in danger of being burned.

The need for death
The people discovered that Sun must be placated by human death, otherwise he could not move. A great chief's wife offered herself. As she did so, her life's breath ebbed away, her body grew cold and then vanished. Whereupon the Sun moved once more. This was the first intimation that every day someone, somewhere in the land, would die. The people were afraid of this prospect until a wise man went to the Place of Emergence and, looking down, saw the dead woman sitting happily by the river of the Fourth World combing her hair. She told him that all the people of the Fifth World must return to live in the Fourth after death. The wise man fell sick soon after this and one night the Moon stood still. The wise man died and Moon continued on its nightly way. Coyote, interpreter of these signs, told the people that, just as every day one of the Navajo must die, so every night someone else, not necessarily a Navajo, must die.

From this interpretation came the belief that death would quickly come to those who gazed on the faces of the dead. Such sights were avoided by covering the faces quickly and by burial. And no Navajo ever ventured to look for the Place of Emergence.

The dispersal of the tribes
When death had been established as essential to the progression of day and night, and as the price of existence in this Fifth World, the tribes of Indians were divided, each resuming its own way of life. Those who had been mountain dwellers in the Fourth World were the mountain tribes of the Fifth; those who had lived in the plains were the plains dwellers. The Navajo remained at the centre, where there was a mountain surrounded by four peaks. In the centre of the land was a small crater lake. They never visited it but adored it from afar as the Place of Emergence. When they first emerged they were no longer able to understand each other. Their language had developed into many separate tongues. It was decided that people with different languages should live in different places.

First Man, First Woman and Coyote were still with the people. But they were not satisfied with the sky. The Sun and Moon alone did not provide sufficient beauty. So they searched for glittering stones and found some mica dust. First Man placed the Star Which Does Not Move at the pole of the heavens. Then he placed the seven stars (Ursa Major) to grow around it. Then he placed the four bright stars at the four quarters of the sky, and designed the groups of stars around them. Next Coyote picked up three shining red pieces of stone and threw them up to become three red dwarf stars. Then in a hurry Coyote scattered the remaining mica dust so it did not fall into exact patterns but scattered the sky with irregular patterns of brilliance.

The three then turned their attention to time, and made the Moon change her shape to mark the seasons. They set out the twelve new moons in front of them and Coyote named them in sequence, and so the year was longer than before when there had been only one Moon.

In the first year of the new time, the world was set in order. For the first time snow fell. It was soft and not cold, and was a very good food. It could be made into wafer bread and eaten. But Coyote felt thirsty, so he put the snow into a pot and melted it over a fire. Ever since then snow has turned into water when it is warmed. First Woman was angry that they had been deprived of the good food. But Coyote told her that she did not understand the purpose of snow. Henceforth snow would melt in the spring and flow down the mountain sides to bring new grass for the animals to eat. It would nourish the fields in which the maize plants and beans would grow fruitfully, and would bring them better food without the labour of hunting and farming. And so it was. Coyote brought seeds of all food plants from the Fourth World and distributed them to the people.

The plagues sent to men
Then there was peace and wealth for all. It should have brought happiness, but the humans were presumptuous and claimed that all happiness was of their own making. They were careless and stupid. First Man and First Woman were unhappy about them, and determined to punish them by creating monsters who would destroy them. There was the giant Yeitso and his children who pursued human prey. Delgeth, the flesh-eating antelope, was made, and the giant who kicked travellers off mountain trails. The People who Killed by Lightning in their Eyes were made: they lived in a house of jewels so beautiful that travellers were tempted to enter and were slain. All these evils were loosed on the people and many men perished.

Now the time came when First Woman felt that man had suffered too much. She was sad in her heart as a mother is sad for a sick child. She went out, and near her mountain of the north-west she found a little girl lying on the ground. She took the child with her to the House of the Northwest. In four days the child grew up. Estanatlehi was her name. She was the means of freedom for the people. As she went walking in the woodlands she saw a handsome man. She told First Man and First Woman but they could see no tracks. But on four successive days she saw him, and lay with him in happiness. Then First Man saw him and knew that he was Sun.

Estanatlehi told her parents that a screen was to be built near the house, so that she could meet Sun in private. For four days Sun visited her there. Then he departed. Four days later the Twin Brothers were born. In four more days they became men, and in another four they decided that they must leave home to seek their father. On the fifth day they went away and met a man in the mountains who told them that Sun dwelt in a land beyond the mountain Tsotsil. So they journeyed on eastwards.

They came to the House of the Sun. It was guarded by the Bear and the Serpent, but they were allowed to pass. Inside the hogan sat the wife of the Sun with her two children. She warned the strangers to leave before

An animal fetish used in rituals designed to make the animals return when game was scarce. It is stuck with precious shells and recalls the myths about the people who lived under the ocean who were supposed to possess special powers. These powers were acquired by Bear and Snake after the raid on the House of Shells, described in the Beauty Chant. Museum of Mankind, London.

the Sun returned. But her two children welcomed the visitors as 'brothers' immediately and, wrapping them in skins, hid them on a shelf. The Sun came home. He heard that two men had come to visit his wife and was angry. He stormed into his hogan demanding to see the visitors. His wife told her children to tell him about them, and when he heard, he pulled down the bundle and the two young men fell out.

The mountains at the corner of the earth were as hard as iron. Sun cast the two young men down on each of the four peaks in turn, but although they were pierced through by the rocks they immediately became whole again. They had been tested in the four directions and now Sun recognised them as his new, deathless sons. Next they must be tested with gifts. He opened the eastern doorway and they beheld limitless herds of horses. They did not desire them. He opened the southern doorway and they beheld mountains of fine clothes. But they desired nothing. He opened the western doorway and they saw jewels of shell and turquoise and coloured stone. They wished for none of them. He opened the northern doorway, and there were all the animals desired by hunters. But they asked for none. Having tested them, he asked them what they desired. They told him that their kinsmen were being devoured by monsters and they wished for magic weapons. They chose a coat studded with iron ore, a great knife, a black and red wind charm and a bundle of thunderbolts.

The Sun told them they must first destroy Yeitso the terrible giant in the east. He warned them that Yeitso was another of his sons, but that he must now be destroyed. Sun would help by depriving Yeitso of his magic armour when the right moment came. Then the Twin Brothers were taken to the sacred sweat bath and purified. Next day father Sun took them under his arms and flew over the world. High in his path he allowed them to look down. They were over the mountain Tsotsil. The elder brother could not recognise the land below, but the younger of the Twins recognised

Tsotsil, the Lake of Salt, and then their home on earth. Then the Sun wrapped them in a thunderstorm and sent them down to the peak of Tsotsil where Yeitso dwelt.

On Tsotsil there was a spring. Every time the giant drank at it he dried it up. There the Twins lay in wait for him. But Tsotsil saw the young men reflected in the water when he came and challenged them and they answered. He cast his thunderbolt at them, but they avoided it and went to another quarter of the peak. Four thunderbolts were cast in the four directions and each time the Twins avoided them. Yeitso had no more thunder power. Then a great black storm overtook them and the great thunder from Sun struck the giant and stripped off his armoured robe. The Twins rushed upon him and attacked him with the big knife. They hacked off his head and threw it into the valley, where it became a rocky hill. Then the blood of the giant began to flow towards it, so with the big knife they cut a ravine so that the blood could not bring the head back to life. The stream of blood halted and turned into a flow of black rock. Then the Twins seized the burnt and shattered armour of the giant and put it into the basket in which he used to carry his victims, and returned to their mother's hogan.

Next day they said they must kill the giant flesh-eating antelope, Delgeth. Estanatlehi their mother, told them it was impossible, for Delgeth lived in the centre of a wide plain where he could see all who approached him. So they decided that they should divide their forces. Elder Twin Brother (Nagenatzani) went to fight the flesh-eater, while Younger Twin Brother (Thobadestchin) stayed to help his mother.

Nagenatzani reached the edge of the plain. He moved among the rocks looking for a way and found none. Then the ground-rat came along and suggested burrowing underground to the centre of the plain. He did this and emerged under the heart of Delgeth. Then he made four burrows radiating from it. Nagenatzani wriggled through the burrow and shot an arrow through the heart of the flesh-eater. In his death throes the antelope ripped up the ground of the burrow where his enemy lay hidden, but Nagenatzani moved to the next burrow. Four times this happened, but in the last burrow Nagenatzani saw the terrible horn rip the ground towards him, stop short and then turn over. He left his hiding place and saw the gigantic carcass. But only when he saw a squirrel scamper over the body was he sure that the monster was dead. The squirrel painted his face red and brown with the blood, and Nagenatzani slit open the carcass and took a length of intestine filled with blood as proof of his victory.

The next struggle was against the great birds who fed their young with human beings. The male devoured men, and came with thunderstorms and lightning flashes. The female destroyed women and came with the female rains, sudden showers that brought no lightning. This pair lived on a high mesa with precipitous sides. They would seize their human victims and drop them from the sky on to a ledge where they were smashed and then devoured by the fledglings in the nest. Nagenatzani offered himself as bait. He carried his thunderbolts and the huge intestine bag filled with blood. The cloud and the thunder came, and the giant bird seized him and hauled him high into the sky before releasing him. The intestine bag hung below him. Swiftly he fell but the bag cushioned his fall. It burst and the blood splashed all around.

Nagenatzani found himself in the nest. Four times the young birds attacked him, and four times he hissed at them and they withdrew. Then he asked them when the parent birds would come back, and learned that they returned with the female rains and the male rains. Suddenly the bodies of two women fell on the ledge and were shattered. A moment later a man's body was broken in the same way. The clouds gathered, there was rain and then thunder over the mesa. The parent birds were returning. The male bird settled on a crag above the eyrie. Nagenatzani cast his thunderbolt at him, and he fell on the rocks

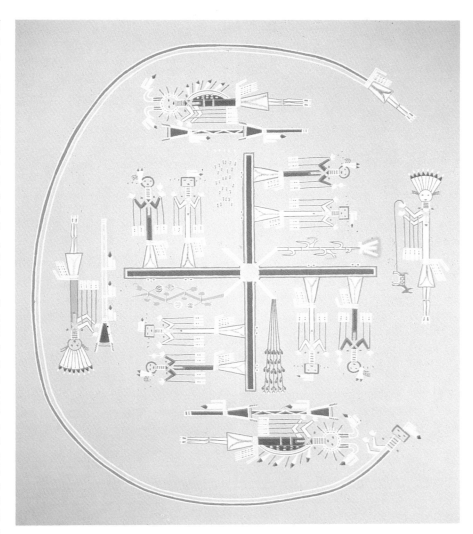

below the nest. Then the mother bird swooped nearer the nest; with another thunderbolt he destroyed her too. Then Nagenatzani picked up the fledglings one by one. The first he threw to the skies and named it Atsa, the eagle. It became full grown at once. He named the others too; they became the various birds of prey.

Now Nagenatzani was alone. He could not fly. He was on a ledge with no way up and no way down. Then far below him he saw Bat-Woman moving. He called for help. Three times she disappeared from view but the fourth time she told him to stand back because he must not see how she came up. He went back to the rock wall and in a few moments Bat-Woman was beside him with her basket on her back. She warned him that he must be prepared to get into her basket and trust her, though he could hardly see the thongs which

held the basket to her back. He must also keep his eyes shut because he must not discover how she flew. He climbed into the basket and covered his eyes. They swooped from the cliff and gently flew down. For a moment he opened his eyes and they began to fall, but Bat-Woman threw her blanket over him and the gentle descent was resumed. They reached the earth.

Then Nagenatzani, from the bodies of the monster birds he had shot down, took the wings for himself and the feathers for Bat-Woman. She valued them greatly, but he warned her that she must not walk over the field of yellow flowers in front of them. But on her way she forgot and started to cross the flower field. Suddenly she heard a twittering and calling in her basket. The feathers had turned into song birds. Bat-Woman was so delighted that she released the birds to make people happy everywhere.

Again the Twins danced with Estanatlehi to record the great victory. But there were yet other trials to be undertaken by Nagenatzani while his brother Thobadestchin helped to cultivate the earth at home.

The Ogre who kicked people off mountain paths was the next to be conquered. He himself never fell because his coarse hair grew into crevices of the rock to hold him. Nagenatzani walked along the path. He extended his wand and the kicker struck out. The young man dodged behind his legs. The kicker was angered. Four times this was done. The kicker danced with rage, then with the big knife Nagenatzani slashed through his hair. As the Ogre crashed, a wailing sound was heard. The hero ran down to find that the kicker had fallen on his wife and family who were now busy cutting up his body and eating it. More birds were made; the Ogre's wife and children were swung into the sky and changed into the carrion eaters.

The last task of Nagenatzani was to go to where the people with the Lightning in their Eyes tempted people into their beautiful palace and then killed them. He took his knife and some salt from the Lake of Salt. Like other visitors he was allowed into the place. But he was the child of the Sun and had thunderbolt protection. He was not stricken. Four times the tempters tried, throwing lightning against him, and each time their eyes stuck out further from their heads. Then he threw the salt on the fire, where it exploded in coruscating yellow flames which burned the eyes of the tempters and made them powerless. He took his big knife and killed and then scalped them. He took the scalps home, and there was a great scalp-dance to celebrate the final victory over the monsters.

Now the only people who were still fulfilling the curse that First Woman and First Man had laid on their people were the descendants of Yeitso the giant. So the Twin Brothers went together to a sacred spot that Sun had told them about. There they put down the black and red wind charm. They danced around it singing magical songs. The winds began to whirl, gathering power until they could uproot and toss great trees about. Then they were directed to the mountains where the enemy lived. The destruction was complete. There were no more giants left.

The work of the Twins Nagenatzani and Thobadestchin was accomplished and all dangers to the human race were ended, though few were left alive after the plagues which First Man and First Woman had released. The Twins took the magical arms back to their father the Sun. But they found Sun was not happy. He was so proud of them that he wished to visit their mother again. He therefore ordered them to return to earth and build two find lodges. In the west was to be the Palace of Estanatlehi, where each day Sun could see her beauty as he came to the end of his journey. At the opposite end of the sky, in the east, were to be the homes of First Man and First Woman, the parents of Estanatlehi. He said he could pass by now without desiring First Woman as he once had, since it was shameful for a man to look on his wife's mother. Thus it was done, and because of this Navajo men would never look at the faces of their mothers-in-law for fear trouble should follow.

The repopulation of the world

Now when all this was done Sun consulted with Nagenatzani and Thobadestchin. They told him that earth was without people; so few were left that they could never repopulate it. Sun told them to explain to their mother that more people were needed and she would know the way to make them. So they returned to Estanatlehi to give her the message.

Their mother took two baskets. One she filled with flour ground from white maize, the other she filled with flour ground from yellow maize. Then she shook her breasts. From the right breast dust fell into the white flour. From the left breast fell dust into the yellow. Then she moulded

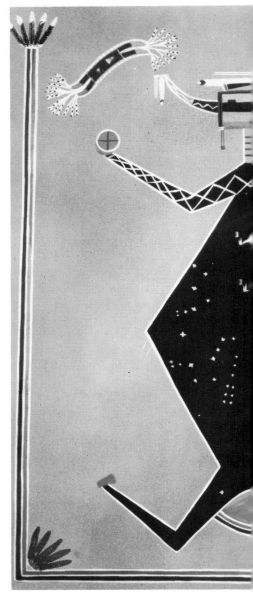

the flour with water into a firm paste. From the white mixture she modelled a man. From the yellow mixture a woman. She warmed them and then placed them under a warm blanket. She watched over them as they lay together all night.

When morning came they were living people. Estanatlehi gave them a special power so that in four days they had children who grew up immediately. The new people, and their children, continued to have children every four days until the country was repopulated again, but stopped before they became as numerous as the ancient peoples had been when they sinned and brought punishment upon themselves. The new people

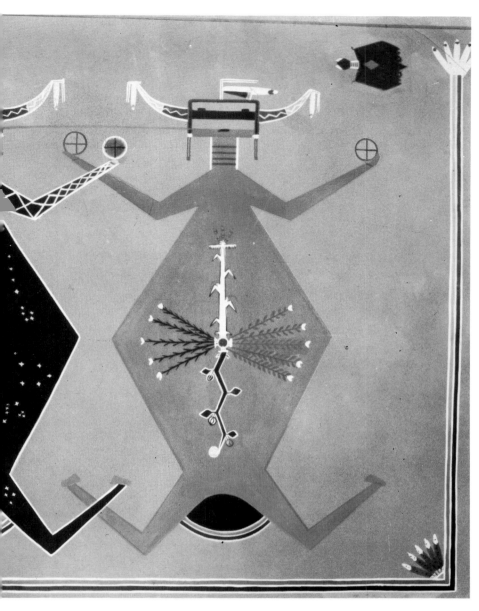

Father Sky and Mother Earth from the Hail Chant. Throughout the southern region of North America the myths speak of these two as the creators of the world and of the race of men. Father Sky is characterised by the stars painted down his front and Mother Earth by the maize symbol. Museum of Navajo Ceremonial Art, Santa Fé, New Mexico.

were placed to live in four houses at the corners of the world. They were the first four clans of the Navajo. Then Estanatlehi began her journey to the House of the West, having decided to create more people. As she went she made four more clans from different coloured maize, taking the skin from the centre of her breasts to mix with the flour. This was believed to be the reason why women had special beauty in their nipples.

The eight people Estanatlehi made on her journey to the House of the West were ancestors of the four new clans that completed the numbers of the Navajo nation. With them the mother sent Bear, Puma and Wild-cat to hunt for them and to protect them.

The world was now completed and people were created to live in it subject to the orders of the gods. Nagenatzani and Thobadestchin went to dwell in a mountain cave near the junction of two rivers, where they are sometimes seen reflected in the waters. Estanatlehi went to her home in the west and became the Goddess of the Sunsetland. She sent everything that was good for the Navajo: the snow, the spring, the summer, the growing plants and maize to cover the hills and valleys. She was much loved by the people. But on the eastern borders of the sky lived her parents, First Man and First Woman. They were envious of the new human race and wanted to send plagues such as

those which destroyed most of the last human race. From them came sickness, wars and the white men.

Another of the Navajo myths recounts the adventures of the sisters who discovered a world of beauty and is called the Beauty Chant. It was used by shamans for curing, and is interesting from a medical point of view because at one point the patient was given a deliberate shock, through the appearance of the shaman acting the return of the Snake-Man near the end of the chant, to help to effect the cure. The greater spirits do not appear in this legend, and its recounting of the activities of animal spirits recalls the legends of simpler people. The world shown here is one where natural powers function in a way similar to that of nature spirits in European classical mythology. The basic difference is that in the European stories the gods have anthropomorphic forms whereas the American Indians use theriomorphic creatures (depicted as beasts) who simply act like humans.

The Beauty Chant

Bear, Snake, Frog and Turtle set out to raid a village of people who lived under the great ocean. Frog and Turtle went alone into one of the hogans, intending to capture a couple of girls alive. The people of the village rushed out and the two adventurers had to kill the girls and take their scalps. The elder girl's hair was decorated with white shell, the younger one's with turquoise. The warriors hid the scalps in their robes and dashed out of the hogan. When the villagers attacked them, Frog made himself small enough to hide inside Turtle's shell, which was so strong that even blows with heavy stone axes failed to break it. Then the villagers decided to throw them into an oven where the fire would destroy them. Turtle was terrified, but Frog was a water creature and squirted water so well that he put the fire out. When the oven was opened up the two creatures emerged unhurt. Then the villagers foolishly threw them into a stream, and both swam to the other shore, where they displayed the scalps with the jewels of the House of Shells.

Now Bear and Snake, who had been look-out men, were told by the wind to go along the coast to meet Frog and Turtle coming up out of the sea.

As they neared home they met eight people from their own village who asked which of them had the scalps. But they refused to say. Two of the villagers, who had daughters at home, said they would give the girls to whoever could shoot farthest. They wished to establish who was strongest so that he might then take the jewelled scalps by force. The eight and the four all shot. All were young except Bear and Snake, who said they were too old to shoot; but all the same they were the winners of the competition. The other ten were so angry that they hurried away leaving Bear and Snake to follow after them. But they did not get far before they were caught up by the elder pair. Three more competitions were held. Each time Bear and Snake were the winners. But no one would let the girls go to them. So the whole party went back to the home village to hold a scalp-dance. This time Bear and Snake did not hurry after the others but camped a little way outside the village and made themselves a shelter of sage-bush.

The people in the village began the scalp-dance, the drums and singing began. All the young people began to dance. The girls were all there, including the two who had been promised as prizes. As they danced the two girls became aware of a strange and wonderful scent. There was no way to find out where it came from except to follow it.

The scent led the girls to the sage-bush shelter, where they were delighted to find two handsome young men. Bear-Man was clothed in black and Snake-Man was coloured like a rainbow. They were bedecked with rich and beautiful jewellery. The elder girl asked Bear for some of the tobacco with the wonderful scent. But he said the young men at the dance would be angry. Snake, however, said they should come inside and then the young women would be allowed to smoke the pipes. The girls, struck by their beauty and kindness, had fallen in love. Bear gave his white shell pipe to the elder girl, and Snake gave his turquoise pipe to the younger. One breath of the smoke each, and they lost consciousness. Next morning they were given incense to revive them. They woke to find the sun was up and Bear and Snake had become old men. The girls were terrified but only the younger girl, Glispa, tried to escape. She found that she was tied to Snake's ankle by a blue racer snake. Whenever she moved he woke up. Whenever she was quiet he slept. She managed to loosen the snake at last and reached the door, only to find an army of snakes all hissing at her. The more frightened she became the more they hissed. Forcing herself to appear calm she walked between them and escaped. After a while she heard human voices, the voices of her relatives from the village. They were very angry and she knew that if she was found they would kill her. She looked back and saw that Snake was chasing her. Quickly she made her way to a river and waded downstream so that she could not be trailed by her scent. When she came to the mountains near the Place of Emergence, she circled round them. She grew thirsty and suddenly there was a lake in front of her. Snake-People came to her gently and asked whence she had come. She told her story. When she had finished, they lifted up the lake, and told her that it was only because she had told the truth that she was allowed to enter their world.

She came to fields of maize and ate. She met Snake-People who offered her bowls of water, and she drank. She found that they lived in adobe houses like the Pueblo people. They invited her into a house in which they assured her she would be safe from the old man. She stayed and was fed with a magical porridge made of pollen, and she found that however much she ate, the bowl never emptied. While she was living here the Snake-Man reappeared at a feast, once more in the form of a young and handsome man, dressed in his all-coloured clothes. Glispa was happy to see that he was young again. She knew that she was happier than ever before, so she laughed with him and ate beside him. He explained that he was a great and powerful shaman who knew the whole of the Hozoni Chant and the accompanying sand-painting rituals. It was a healing chant and she learnt it very quickly. For two years she lived with the Snake-People and was happy. Then she became homesick. Snake said that the time was come when she should visit her people and teach the Hozoni Chant to her brother so that he could bring healing to his people.

So Glispa returned to her people. Any fears she had were unfounded.

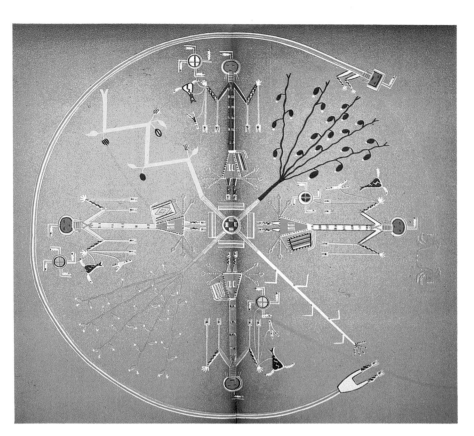

Opposite. Navajo sand-painter at Gallup, New Mexico.

Above. This painting of a sand-painting appeared in a publication in 1883–4. Sand-paintings were made during the performance of a ceremonial chant or song, and erased at the end of the ceremony.

Above. Apache devil dance masks, worn by dancers representing mountain spirits during the girls' initiation ceremony. White River, Arizona. American Museum of Natural History, New York.

Opposite. Navajo mask of Hastsobaka, 'Chief made God'. Used in Yei-be-chai, a healing rite. Made of painted hide, cotton cloth, shells and wood. Cottonwood Pass, Arizona. The Brooklyn Museum, New York.

Time had passed and their anger was forgotten, they welcomed her as one returned from the dead. She tried to teach her brother how to perform the healing ceremonies, but he could not remember the sequence of movements or the colours when making the sand-paintings.

After a time Glispa took some fine maize kernels, and as she sang the chants and directed his hands she laid a single kernel at each important point. Four kernels marked each song. Then they were left all night in the rows as she had laid them. Next morning maize was gathered and boiled into a gruel. Then she had a captive slave bring the food in a basket specially woven for the ceremony. After her brother had eaten the gruel his memory no longer failed him. He learned all the ceremonies, the chants, the sand-

paintings and the feather prayer-offerings. Glispa sang ceremonies over her brother with herbs, trees and sand and he became a great shaman and acquired power to initiate others whom he knew to be fitted for the office.

The celebration of the Beauty Chant, by the Navajo, lasted four days and four nights while the people took ritual steam baths to symbolise their cleansing from the ignorant past. As the nocturnal ceremonies were nearing their conclusion the return of Snake-Man was described. At this point the shaman, disguised as Snake-Man, would suddenly appear. This was intended to shock the patient, and thus cure him, probably with the suggestion that this might be the serpent calling him to the underworld, just as in the myth Snake-Man had called Glispa to return to the world beneath the lake.

The Beauty Chant, like many others, had the specific purpose of bringing health and well-being to those for whom it was performed. The Emergence Myth was of still greater power. Its recital could heal the sick, initiate the aspirant to religious experience, and unite the people with the world of nature. In effect, the ancient chants of the Navajo people were a form of psychotherapy which helped the sick to heal their divided spirit or to reclaim their missing soul (for sickness was thought of as a matter of the spirit more than of the body).

This linking of the myths with healing ceremonies were probably the major factors in preserving them. Both onlookers and participants felt that they themselves were involved in the myths, and that their integration with the world of nature and with the spirits was thereby renewed. In its own way the ritual must have conveyed an emotional balance similar to that attained through regular participation in the religious ceremonies of the more complex civilisations of Europe and Asia.

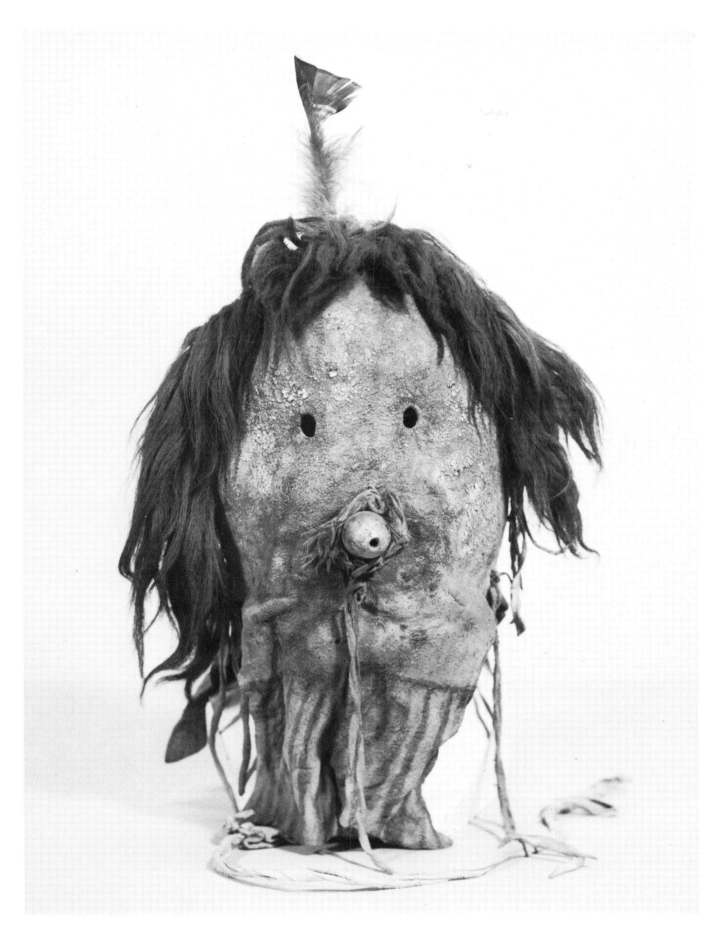

The Farmers of the Southeastern Woodlands

The southern part of the United States from the Atlantic Coast to the Mississippi could, in prehistoric times, boast the highest development of Indian civilization north of Mexico. The most spectacular features of the archaeology of this region are the many large and complex earthworks which have led to the term 'Mound Builder' being applied to the culture of the prehistoric eastern tribes. The ceremonial centres and chiefs' houses of the Mound Builders were wooden constructions raised on great earth mounds, some in the form of sacred animals. The art of these people ranks high in the field of small stone sculpture and engraving on shell and copper. Their culture did not disappear suddenly, but became weakened in time, leaving reflections of its glory among neighbouring tribes.

In the days of King James I (1603-25) a crew of English sailors engaged in a raid on the coast of Mexico were captured by the Spaniards and jailed in Mexico City. Most of them died under torture or were executed, but five men escaped from prison and proceeded to walk across North America. They were picked up by an English ship on the New England Coast. Unfortunately, they were taken to be questioned by the English authorities about their adventures, in case they could give military information useful in the wars with Spain,

A reconstructed Seminole Indian village in the Florida Everglades.

and to ensure their uninhibited replies they were stretched on the rack. Apparently they had some idea of what was expected and told a satisfyingly detailed story of their journey through the Natchez, Creek and Choctaw country in which they had seen fine palaces of timber and stone built on huge earth mounds and decorated with pearls and diamonds, people wearing fine clothes and jewels, and plates made of gold everywhere. In the first edition of his great work on the voyages of English navigators Hakluyt quoted their short account in the Star Chamber records, but in the second edition he omitted it as altogether incredible. However, it seems to have been an exaggeration of real facts; the jewels were nothing more than lovely smoky river pearls like those which a Cherokee princess offered to the Spanish explorer De Soto, and the plates of gold described sometimes existed, although there was, no doubt, much more of copper. As to the marvellous accounts of empires, the truth is represented by the loose confederation of the Creek towns and the small *imperium* of the Natchez whose eight towns included those of two subject tribes. One could

wish that somewhere among the records of Elizabethan and Jacobean travels there had been some less ingenious account than that told by men who had suffered greatly under the Inquisition, travelled far across mountains and forests only to be racked for information at home.

The historic tribes

Although the decline of the Mound-Builder culture began long before the European impact, some Indian groups, such as the Natchez, still retained some features of this civilization when first encountered by European explorers. The Natchez may indeed have descended directly from the Mound Builders. They alone among historical North American Indian tribes had a sacred king, called the 'Great Sun', whose power was absolute. He wore elaborate feather capes and crowns, and was carried everywhere in a litter.

The entire Southeast was strongly affected by European settlement. Entire tribes became extinct through wars and new diseases. Others, like the so-called Five Civilized Tribes – the Cherokee, Choctaw, Creek, Chickasaw and Seminole – quickly

adopted the ways of their white neighbours. In spite of this, peaceful co-existance proved impossible, and by the 1830s most of the Five Civilized Tribes had been moved to Oklahoma, leaving only a few scattered groups in the Southeast.

The Natchez became involved in struggles against the French, and the final tragedy came when the French granted land, which included the site of the chief and sacred town of the Natchez, to French settlers for use as plantations. They saw only a poor wooden village built on ramps of earth, which was all that remained after nearly a century of intermittent wars with the white men. After the final desperate battles, the remaining 700 Natchez were sent to settle among neighbouring tribes. They preserved some of their old traditions in a weakened and distorted form. As their numbers decreased and knowledge of their old language faded, the ancient traditions became confused. When anthropologists recovered accounts of the myths from the last few speakers of the old tongue, they gathered mixed and distorted legends. The same process is reflected in Britain, in the way that the sacred

Left. A death's head effigy jar from a mound in Mississippi County, Arkansas. The incised decoration, which represents the traditional body-painting, shows Aztec influence. Museum of the American Indian, Heye Foundation, New York.

Opposite. The many mounds in the form of birds, bears and other animals, found in the Mississippi and Ohio regions are relics of a civilisation which flourished in North America about two thousand years ago. The Great Serpent Mound is 1350 feet (412 metres) long, and is therefore the largest. It is situated in Adams County, Ohio.

Left. A kneeling man carved in stone from Temple Mound, Tennessee. It was placed as an offering in the mound and may be a figure of a hero. At this period (AD 1000-1600) the Indians erected large mounds on which they built wooden temples in which stone figures such as this were placed. Metropolitan Museum of Art, New York.

The flyer.

Celtic chant to the Lady of the Underworld has become the nursery rhyme 'Sing a Song of Sixpence'.

A similar, but much less complete, process affected the development of Creek myths. The loose confederation of villages broke up on contact with white settlers, but the main tribal ceremonies were preserved by the Creeks and the language kept alive. Much was saved by the efforts of the Creeks themselves. An important aspect of their handling of new experiences was the process of gradual assimilation. They absorbed many folk tales heard from the European settlers into their mythology, and many acquired from the negro slaves from West Africa. The Creeks in turn had a considerable influence on negro folk tales, especially in the imposition of their own concept of the Trickster Spirit, personified as the Rabbit, on to the cycle of Ashanti stories about Anansi, the Trickster. In Jamaica Anansi suffers a spelling change and is often called Nancy, but in the south eastern United States he took over the name of his Creek Indian archetype and has since charmed the world as Brer Rabbit.

The coming of fire

The following account of Rabbit comes from a Hitchiti Indian myth. He is the Trickster of the legend describing the coming of fire and is very like Raven in the stories of the Indians of the Northwest Coast. Although the stories are different, the relationships are the same. The degeneration of myth has made it into a confused tale about 'people' instead of about the Sky People and the First People on the earth below, but the detail of the myth makes the identification clear.

A dance was to take place on the village square where the Sky People were going to celebrate Puskitá, the Green Corn Festival of purification. They would make fire afresh. The dancing square was the only place where one was allowed to make fire. But Rabbit thought there should be fire in other places. He thought for a long time. Then he had his friends rub his head with pine until his hair

stood on end. Everyone thought his new crested headdress looked so fine that they made him leader of the dance.

The dancers followed him, circling the four directions of the sacred fire logs. As they passed the east, Rabbit bent low, as if to throw the offerings of tobacco to the fire. People said that when Rabbit danced he always acted extravagantly, and did not notice how low he bent. On the fourth round he set his headdress on fire, and ran away so fast that they failed to catch him. Then the people worked magic and made a great rain which lasted four days. They thought the stolen fire would be put out by then and allowed the sun to shine again. Rabbit, however, had run into a hollow tree and made a fire there in shelter, emerging when the sun shone. So again the people made rain. Every time Rabbit came out he lit new fires, but the rain put most of them out. The First People saw these fires and were quick to light firebrands at them. After this they had fires in their homes, and whenever the rains put them out the people who had fire shared it with the others. In the end the rains stopped, everybody was allowed to have fire, and Rabbit was remembered for bringing fire to the Hitchiti.

The origin of tobacco

The culture of the Indians of the Southeast contained varying attitudes to many of the myths, mainly because climatic and economic influences were different from those in other regions. The origin of tobacco is an example. In the plains, where it was not native, it was a marvellous star plant. But in the Southeast tobacco was linked with sex to account for its power of giving peace.

A young man and a girl travelling together fell in love and left the path for the happiness of intercourse. They were so pleased that they agreed to marry. Later, on a hunting journey, the man returned to the place where they had first united and there found a pretty flower with scented leaves. He took it back to the people and told of the discovery. They said, 'When it

Above. An incised conch shell from the Spiro Mound, Oklahoma. It portrays an eagle man and probably represents a ceremonial dancer, AD 1200-1600. Museum of the North American Indian. Heye Foundation, New York.

Opposite. 'The Flyer', a watercolour by John White, 16th century. Museum of Mankind, London.

is dried, we will smoke it, and name it "Where We Came Together."' The elders of the tribes claimed that because the man and woman were so completely at peace and happy when tobacco was made it has been smoked ever since at councils for promoting peace and friendship between the tribes.

The origin of maize

This is another story in which some elements of the world above the earth have been applied to people of the present world. It has, however, preserved most of its simplicity. It attributes the origin of maize to the creative female magic of an old woman who must have been some kind of earth-mother goddess.

An old woman lived alone. She trod her own paths from the house until they were smooth. One day, on one of the paths, she saw a clot of blood. She covered it with a jar. Later she removed the jar and found a baby boy underneath. When he grew up he called her Grandmother. When he was seven she made him his first bow and arrows. He went out with them and came back full of questions.

'What is it, Grandmother, that has a bushy tail and runs up trees?' 'It is a squirrel. Shoot it and bring it home to eat.' He did so. Then he went out again. 'What is it that flies from tree to tree?' 'It is a bird and good to eat. Shoot it and bring it home.' And another day, 'I saw a big animal with big feet and its body leaning forward. It had no tail and its ears were round. What can it be?' 'That is a bear and good to eat. Shoot it and bring it home.' By asking these questions, day after day, he named all the food animals.

Now he went hunting everywhere, but Grandmother told him he must never pass a distant blue mountain on the horizon. He hunted many things but never discovered from which creature his Grandmother made the *sofky* maize gruel and the blue dumplings of maize and beans. He knew nothing of plants. He decided one day to peep in through the door when she was preparing food. He saw her remove her dress and straddle a corn

sieve. As she scratched one of her thighs, a stream of maize poured down. As she scratched the other thigh, a stream of beans descended. When he came in and would not eat, the Grandmother guessed that he had discovered her secret. She told him that now he had solved the mystery he must leave her and go beyond the blue mountain. To protect him, she made a magical headdress of intertwined rattlesnakes and blue jay-birds which rattled and sang when he put it on.

Now Grandmother told him that all was ready for his journey. He must marry the first girl that he met, and then return. As he left he was to shut the door, with Grandmother inside, and set fire to the house so that nothing would remain but ashes. He did so and the fire consumed everything just as Grandmother had decreed.

The Orphan Boy went out over the mountains. He came to a village where men were playing a ball game. They stopped to watch him with his marvellous headdress of rattlesnakes and blue-jays. Rabbit was there, and he said he would walk along the path with him. They came to a lake where there were many turtles. Rabbit said, 'Come! When I say "jump" we will dive in and each catch some turtles.' Orphan Boy agreed. Rabbit called out 'Jump'. Orphan Boy set his marvel-

lous headdress beside the lake and jumped in. Rabbit snatched the hat and ran away as fast as he could.

Orphan Boy caught his turtles. The men were sorry for him when he told of his loss and brought him to the village. There he entered the first house and was welcomed by a beautiful young woman. He made a hole near her house and put the turtles in it. He returned and she accepted him as her husband. Next he saw her mother and told her, 'There are turtles in the ground. Go and bring some, and cook for us all.' She followed his directions and found many fine turtles. In this way Orphan Boy proved that he was a good provider.

Soon Rabbit was brought in, having been seized for stealing the magical headdress. It had neither rattled nor sung since Rabbit stole it, but, as soon as Orphan Boy touched it, the rattlesnakes buzzed their rattles and the bluejays sang. Rabbit asked to be thrown among the dogs. The tribespeople thought that this would certainly make an end of him, but as soon as he was thrown amongst them, the dogs went to sleep and Rabbit ran off unharmed, ready for further mischief.

One day Orphan Boy took his wife to the river. He told her that if he could swim across four times they would be able to catch enough fish

Above. Shell mask from the Brakebill Mound, Tennessee. Masks like this were cut from large white ocean shells and are found throughout the south-east area. They are commonly found in graves and were probably used either as masks to cover the faces of the dead or as amulets to hang round their necks. Peabody Museum, Harvard University, Cambridge, Massachusetts.

Left. Thought to be a fragment of a temple hanging. It was brought back to England by an early explorer and is known as Powhatan's mantle, though there is no evidence that it ever did belong to the southeastern chief of that name. The shell decoration is typical of North American Indian art. Ashmolean Museum, Oxford.

Opposite, left. A stone mask from Tennessee. Masks such as this, which were too heavy to be worn, and which have no eye apertures, were probably used to cover the faces of the dead. Some of the southern tribes believed that if one looked on the faces of the dead, one's own death would be hastened. Cincinnati Art Museum, Ohio.

Opposite, right top. A sandstone pipe-bowl from a mound in Boone County, Kentucky. It shows old mother frog who played a part in the creation of the world in many southern myths. Museum of Mankind, London.

Opposite, right bottom. Tobacco smoking was part of the ceremonial life of the southern tribes of North America because it was believed to promote peace and friendship. This ancient stone pipe comes from a mound in McMinnville, Tennessee. It represents the Great Turtle who was believed to support the world. Museum of Mankind, London.

for all the people of the village. She believed him and called all the people. He swam across four times and hundreds of fine big fish came up for them. Rabbit was envious and said he would do the same and swam across four times. The fish appeared, but all so dead that their eyes had turned white and their bodies rotten. The people chased Rabbit out of the village and warned him never to come back.

Having provided for the villagers, Orphan Boy and his wife went on the journey over the mountains, back to the place where Grandmother had

been burnt. There they found the ground covered by a fine crop of maize plants and beans. Each maize plant was wearing a skirt of earth around its base, and that is why the Indians subsequently made little skirts of earth for their maize seed to sprout through. They believed that maize was really old Grandmother.

The flood

The myths of the Creek Indians have changed less than those of the once mighty Natchez. Some of the original content of the Natchez myths still survives, but gives the impression that many of the legends have been mixed. In the flood story that follows, there are three social groups of people among the survivors. They probably represent the Suns, the Nobles, and the Commoners of ancient Natchez society, but the myth provides no clue as to the origin of the social differentiation although this was probably explained in the original.

The story tells of the Dog who warned his master to make a raft because all things would be overwhelmed by a flood. As the water rose the Dog and the Man saw the mountains burst open and strange monsters emerge. But the waters drowned everything except Man and Dog, lifting them above the clouds where they saw a wonderful world of land and trees. But Dog told Man that he must return to the place he had come from and that this would be impossible unless he threw Dog into the flood. Much against his will, Man threw Dog into the waters and they began to subside. Dog warned Man not to land until the ground had had seven days in which to dry. When this had happened Man saw people coming to him because he still had fire on the raft. Some were naked, some wore rags and some wore beautiful clothes. The three groups divided the fire between them. Then a noise was heard in the east and an Old Man appeared to say that although their bodies had been dead for various periods they would continue to live in spirit.

The myth reflects the Natchez custom of drying the bodies of the dead and keeping them on frames in sacred buildings. There are similarities between this myth and a longer story about the seventh son of a cannibal giant who had already destroyed six sons. The seventh son escaped and jumped up a tree in the night. When morning came he was terrified to discover that the tree was really a horn of the great water serpent who was now swimming up the river. Canoes loaded with deformed people drifted by. They all laughed at him because he was riding on the serpent. But at last a canoe full of girls drew alongside him. They were sorry for him, and told him to spit towards them. He did so and they came nearer until he was able to board the boat.

The canoe continued on its course along the great river for so long a period that he married one of the girls, who bore his child while they travelled on. They came at last to where the seventh son's mother lived. At first she hid from him, doubting his identity because she lived in darkness and all kinds of animals, especially the rats, came to her pretending to be her son. But when she saw her grandchild she danced for joy and led all three to the place of a great chief.

The chief had many wives but he always blinded them. When he saw his visitors arrive he prepared to welcome them. The old mother had taken command. She would not approach the chief unless he made his wives all lie down to make a pathway for them. So he ordered the wives to lie side by side. Then the old mother became young again and led her son and grandson over the women. The chief married the mother, but the son did not want her eyes removed and the chief had him thrown out. When the son returned her eyes had been removed. The son set them back in their sockets but the chief had her eyes removed a second time. On his return he found her dancing blind before the chief who was beating a magic drum. The young man restored his mother's eyes again, desparately seized the magic drum and rushed his family to the canoe. The chief and his

TOMBEAUX des Rois de la VIRGINIE.

blind wives were unable to stop them and the family escaped, with the son beating the magic drum, towards the west.

This story is possibly an account of a voyage through the stars and a visit to the underworld. The principal characters are probably Moon (the mother), Sun (the chief) and Morning Star (the son).

The Rolling Heads

The North American Indians as a whole had an obsessive ghost story about heads with no bodies, the Rolling Heads. The story is to be found in almost every tribe, though there are local variations. The Natchez version of this takes place in the warm swampy terrain of their homeland. It has a definite mythological character, although confused by the lapse of time. The hero and heroine seem to have control over the powers of nature, and it is probably another myth about the Moon and the Morning and Evening Stars. The characters have many adventures which finally end in the trapping of the destructive power.

Two brothers lived together. One day a woman came and said she wanted to live with them. They decided that she should be the wife of Younger Brother. Later the brothers went out fishing. A big fish came up. The only way they could think to catch it was for Elder Brother to tie a hickory-bark rope round Younger Brother, throw him into the water, and drag him ashore with the fish in his arms. They tried this, but the fish was too big and swallowed Younger Brother, snapping off the rope. Elder Brother ran along the bank asking the animals to help him. With the excep-

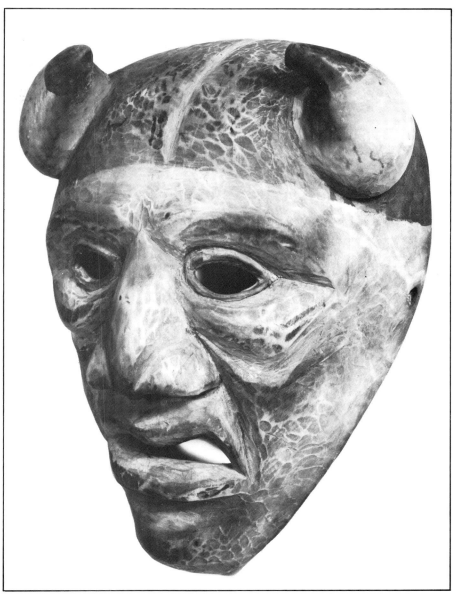

tion of Kingfisher they were all terrified of the fish and ran away. Kingfisher perched on the fish and hammered with his long bill on its side until it died and drifted to the bank. There Elder Brother cut it open; but only the head of Younger Brother remained, the rest of him had been reduced to powder. The head spoke, instructing Elder Brother to wash it well and place it on a log. The head said that he would visit the house in the morning and would sing as the sun came up, and his wife was to be warned he could not longer act as her husband.

That night Elder Brother took the woman as his wife. Next morning the head flew through the air and sat on the roof singing. On hearing that Elder Brother had taken his wife, Younger Brother plotted to kill him. The head asked them to come out to pluck fruit from the trees. It then flew to a tree and began to eat the fruit, throwing the skins at the woman to provoke Elder Brother to climb after him, but Crow warned them to escape while they were able.

Elder Brother and the woman fled.

But the head saw them and came rolling along the ground, screaming at them. They ran for the house of the Mud-wasp, where the head, in close pursuit, demanded that the woman should be handed over. The Mud-wasp denied that she was there, but the head could not be deceived, he had already seen the imprint of the woman's buttocks where she had slipped in the mud.

Mud-wasp then told the woman to lie down. He took her genitals and, with a few magical cuts, changed her into a man. To confuse the head he took the two men outside asking them to show their skill by shooting a row of four pots. The New Man's arrows pierced all four. But Elder

Above. Shell gorget representing a warrior apparently dancing with the head of his victim. Castalian Springs, Sumner County, Tennessee. AD 1200-1600. Museum of the American Indian, Heye Foundation, New York.

Opposite. The image of the head with antlers is one of the oldest, and most widespread, of man's symbols. This example comes from the Spiro Mound, Oklahoma. It is carved in one piece and inlaid with shells. It was probably worn at the Deer Ceremony to promote good hunting. AD 1200-1600. Museum of the American Indian, Heye Foundation, New York.

Brother pierced only one. The head was convinced by this that the better shot was a man also. He invited the New Man to hunt deer with him. When he saw the manner in which the other hunted his suspicions returned and he renewed the chase. They came to a swampy creek. The head suggested that they should jump in and swim across. The New Man leapt in with the head. Underwater he sang a charm which told the Rolling Head that this was his home and he should stay there. Then he turned back into a woman and escaped, leaving the head imprisoned beneath the waters of the creek.

As she continued her journey she found she was pregnant. She gave birth to several babies, which she put in the joints of a big bamboo that she carried with her. She came to the house of a chief, who married her because she was so attractive, although he already had many wives. She became his favourite. This made the others ashamed and angry. They challenged her to a contest to see who

could make the most parched maize. She went to her old friend the Mud-wasp for advice and he told her to open the top joint of her cane. When he did so Kingfisher flew out. While the other wives were working hard, Kingfisher went to all the villages and collected parched maize for her and so she won the contest.

Next, to test her attractiveness, the other wives proposed a contest to discover which of them had the most beautiful pubic hair. Again she was advised to open a joint of the cane. This time Humming Bird flew out, and wove the iridescent down of humming-bird breasts into her hair. Once again she triumphed. She was then challenged to play a ball game. The rival wives decided that while the game was in progress they would attack and kill her with their shinny sticks. Friendly Mud-wasp said she must now open the whole cane and let out all her children. She did so, and living creatures came streaming out. Among them were storm and thunder, who swirled the dust in the air and confused the women, and lightning, who struck them down.

In triumph and with all her children around her, the woman went on her way, and as she travelled she sent her offspring out in different directions to people the earth as she followed her path westwards.

This myth from the warm swampland of the Natchez country contains some of the elements found in the myths of the Creek tribes: the journey, the danger threatening a particular woman (Moon), the hostility of a chief (Sun) or his wives and the woman's rescue by her children (Stars). Its confused nature is typical of the myths that have survived in which the original distinctions have been blurred by the passage of time. The stories themselves speak only of 'people' although it is possible to indicate the Sky People, First People and spirits of the natural world who must have featured in the original myths and it is unlikely that we shall ever know their exact form. In contrast, the myths of the desert Indians are the best preserved of any.

The Dwellers on the Mesas

In the Southwest region the most highly organised Indian communities lived in large villages called 'pueblos' (meaning 'towns') by the first Spanish explorers. The villages were built on the mesas, the high rocky tableland typical of this area. Some of the villages were built of stone, others of adobe, formed of sun-dried mud bricks. The present-day Pueblo Indians live in northern Arizona and New Mexico, but in pre-Columbian times their villages were scattered from the plains of Texas to the desert wastes of Nevada and southwards as far as northern Mexico.

Although divided by language into four distinct groups, the Pueblo Indians shared a common culture. Their distinctive civilisation had been forced on them by the necessities of their situation. In the 11th and 12th centuries the fertile lands where they had grown their food were devastated by increasing drought. Raids by nomadic tribes from the north increased and the settled communities were forced to find easily defensible spots from which they could emerge to cultivate the remaining fields whenever possible. After a period of cliff-dwelling the towns were moved to commanding sites on the flat-topped mesas. Each was near a watering place and the people went out daily to cultivate their plantations. Often the cultivated plots were some miles distant from the towns, so in periods of danger the warriors went out to protect the women at their work.

The Pueblo tribes were of mixed origin. Some had been settled cultivators in pre-drought times, while others were remnants of simpler people from the west who found it

A view of Zuñi *c.* 1908. The chamber on
the left, with ladder-poles projecting from
the hatchway in the kiva of the north.
Many dances were performed in the
small plaza shown here. Note the sheep
dung piled against one of the houses
which was used for firing pottery.
Photographed by E. S. Curtis.

safer to live with their neighbours rather than fight them. The mixture is evident in their myths as well as in some local differences within a particular linguistic group.

Life in the pueblo

Considerable social organisation was needed for the Pueblo way of life. Under desert growing conditions, gathering and storing food was always a communal concern. Each family looked after its own livelihood, but they banded together for protection. Each family group was required to maintain reserves of grain, so that if the crops failed in any one year, there would be approximately half rations available from stored reserves kept in huge baskets and pottery vessels.

This way of life was reflected in the agglomeration of family apartments which made the town one large complex of solid building with several large multi-storied houses arranged around one or more courtyards or plazas, so that the single-room dwellings were clustered together like cells in a three- or four-tiered beehive. Access to the upper stories was provided by wooden ladders which

could be drawn up in time of danger.

Underneath the courtyards lay the underground chambers known as kivas, which were entered through a hole in the floor. These were the meeting rooms of the various religious societies, some organised on a clan basis, some dedicated to the service of particular spiritual powers. In the kivas the tribe held its religious ceremonies, usually for men only, and arranged their outdoor activities, such as the processions of masked and costumed dancers, impersonating and inspired by the kachinas. 'Kachina' is the name given to several kinds of supernatural being – animal spirits, tribal ancestors and natural forces, such as rain, wind, cloud and thunder. The exact number of these beings is unknown, but at least 500 appear in the mythologies of the different villages.

Each of the religious societies had a leader, and the various clan groups had chiefs. Government was conducted through meetings of a council of elders rather than by dictatorship of any one group. Women occupied a respected place in society and descent was normally through the female line. Pueblo towns often had dependent villages and were, in effect, independent communities who traded a little between themselves and sometimes united to repel raids by the more aggressive tribes from the Plains. But, in the main, the Pueblo Indians were peaceful and sought to occasion no hatred from neighbouring peoples.

Pueblo crafts

Some of the most impressive products of Pueblo craftsmanship are the items made in connection with religious ceremonies, such as the elaborately painted and decorated leather masks worn by the kachina dancers. Stone or wood fetishes are carved for a variety of religious usages by most of the Pueblo groups, but, in general, sculpture is not highly developed in this area.

Weaving is an old Pueblo craft. In early times, the principal material, a type of native cotton, was grown to be spun. After the introduction of

Above. Present-day view of a pueblo in Taos, New Mexico.

Opposite left. Hopi dance wand with a painted kachina figure, decorated with feathers and maize-stalks. Pueblo dances were the dramatised expression of a prayer to the spirits and were formal, elaborate and disciplined. Metropolitan Museum of Art, New York.

Opposite, right. Drawing of Eototo, a kachina from the Hopi pueblo of Walpi. Eototo played an important part in the celebrations that marked the depature of the kachinas, for they were believed to be absent from the people for half of the year. Smithsonian Institution, Washington, D.C. Bureau of American Ethnology.

Feather prayer sticks from a Zuñi pueblo.
They were carried in the prayer
ceremonies to symbolise the link between
the spirits and man, which was marked
by the sacrifice of an eagle every year.
Museum of Mankind, London.

then rubbing the surface smooth.
After firing, they are decorated with
painted designs in various combi-
nations of red, orange, white and
black.

The pictorial arts were highly
formalised. Traditional figures
painted in mineral colours decorated
ceremonial boards, the walls of kivas,
and the masks and headdresses worn
by the dancers who impersonated the
kachina spirits in the ceremonies.

Among the Pueblo Indians we find
a civilisation which in its early stages
developed in comparative isolation.
After the initial Spanish invasion their
struggles were on a small scale and
conditions were ameliorated by the
Spanish missions. Yet these struggles
were nonetheless bitter, involving
much cruelty on both sides and
helped to perpetuate the isolation of
the Pueblo Indians through a repu-
tation for recklessness and cruelty
which they hardly deserved. In
modern times contact with other
areas of the United States, although
sometimes unsuccessful, has led to
increasing understanding and helpful-
ness on both sides, and during the
last half-century the arts of the Pueblo
Indians have made a considerable
impression on artistic taste in the USA
The religious dances and processions
of the kachinas have become more
and more a tourist show, but there
have also been intellectual contacts
between Indian elders and anthropologists which have resulted in the preservation in literary form of much of
the ancient tradition.

The myths that follow show the
distinctive Pueblo Indian character of
their mythology, for the archetypal
deities dress and behave as Pueblo
Indians. Projected unconsciously
from the Indians' own hearts, the
deities appear to them as visionary
beings who have the power of giving
blessings and receiving love. What
follows is the beginning of the story
of creation as told in the town of
Zuñi, in northwest New Mexico,
round about 1880.

The creation of the world
Before creation began there was only
the 'one who contains everything',

sheep by the Spanish settlers, wool
was used as embroidered decoration
on cotton garments. As well as
everyday clothing, kilts, belts and
sashes had to be woven for
ceremonial wear. Throughout the
Pueblo area, weaving was man's
work. The elaborate leggings and
shirts of the men, and the dresses and
shawls of the women of more recent
times, evolved through contact with
the outside world. Yet the people
were not without beauty in the earlier
times. They decorated their woven
garments with rich vegetable dyes,
painted themselves for ceremonies
and worked with turquoise and shell
to produce beautiful jewellery. These
ornaments were primarily of symbolic
value, but were also worn for their
beauty and for the emotional
wellbeing which they brought.

Pottery, the greatest of all the
prehistoric crafts of this area in terms
of variety and quantity, is still an
activity in the Southwest, in spite of
a break in the tradition following the
Spanish conquest. Pots are made by
pinching coils of clay together and

Awonawilona; otherwise, there was blackness and nothingness. Awonawilona created life within himself; the mists of increasing and the streams of growing flowed from him. He assumed a form and was the maker of light, the sun. When the sun appeared the mists gathered together and fell as water, becoming the sea on which the world floats. From within himself Awonawilona formed seed and impregnated the waters. Then, in the warmth of the sun, green scum formed over the great waters and became solid and strong. It was divided and became Earth Mother of the Four Directions and Sky Father who covers everything.

Earth and Sky lay in union and the fourfold womb of Earth conceived all creatures. Then Earth Mother separated from Sky. She would not give birth; all must be prepared. So Earth and Sky assumed the forms of man and woman and discussed the creation of the earth. Earth Mother held a bowl of water and described how the mountains should be made to divide land from land, and stand around the rim of the world. She spat into the water and stirred it with her fingers making foam arise. She drew milk from her breasts to give it life. So she indicated the coming of life, and showed how children should be nourished. She breathed upon the foam, and mists and rainbows arose as clouds floating above the sea. Then Sky breathed and rain fell from the clouds. This showed how man would find warmth and life near Earth Mother and cold from Sky Father, whose breath would bring fertilising rain to Earth again. The Indians believed that because of this, warmth ever remains with women and coldness strengthens men. The Sky Father opened his hand. Within every crease there lay innumerable grains of shining maize. In his thumb and

A witchcraft fetish jar from a Zuñi pueblo. It was used in a ceremony held for the punishment and purification of witches. When not in use the fetishes, carved from elk and deer antlers, were kept inside the bowl and 'fed' with sacred corn meal through the circular hole near the bottom. Museum of the American Indian, Heye Foundation, New York.

Above, left. The Pueblo Indians were fond of ornaments made from turquoise and shell. The shell was worn as an amulet in the winter solstice ceremony. Zuñi pueblo. Museum of Mankind, London.

Above, right. A bird carved in black basalt inlaid with turquoises, from a Zuñi pueblo. The Pueblo Indians included birds and animals in their creation myth about the journey made to the Place of Emergence. Taylor Museum, Colorado Springs Art Center.

Opposite. A Smoki ceremonial. In each pueblo (village) there were one or more kivas – underground rooms, often entered through a hole in the roof. They provided a meeting place for the many religious societies and some of the ceremonies were held there.

forefinger he took some of the shining grains and placed them in the sky as brillant stars to be a guide to humans when the bright sun was hidden. They marked the six regions of the sky in which stars would move: north, south, east, west, upwards and downwards. Then he blessed the breasts of Earth Mother, saying that the golden grains would spring from her to be food for their children.

Then Earth Mother and Sky Father parted and assumed their cosmic forms again. Within the innermost of the four wombs, the Place of Generation, life began to quicken. The beginnings of creatures were formed, dark, horrible and writhing in the darkness. They had neither knowledge nor cleanliness and crawled over one another crying for escape to a better world. As time passed they became wiser and more like the form they were finally to have. Among them was One Alone, the sacred master Poshaiyangkyo, who was able to escape. He found a path from the inner womb and followed it, where no one else could go, outwards and

upwards until he came to the light. There in the swamp of creation, wallowing in the waters, he came seeking the sun and praying for the beings still imprisoned.

Sun Father cast his beams down upon the foam around the earth. He impregnated this Foam Mother and she give birth to twins, the Preceder and the Follower, of the right hand and the left. Sun Father imparted to them some of his wisdom. He also gave them gifts: their mother the Foam Cloud, the rainbow, the thunderbolts and the fog-shield that makes clouds.

The blessed Twins were given dominion as if they were creators ruling all creatures. They used the rainbow to raise Sky Father above the earth so that warmth could come to the surface. Then they flew towards the road of Poshaiyangkyo, and the Place of Generation. They cleft the earth with the thunderbolts and, being small, they descended on threads of spider-web. They came to the deep inner womb where they went among the developing creatures to instruct them and lead them from womb to womb until they could be born on the earth.

When all the creatures were ready the Preceder and the Follower found grass, vines and trees and bound them together to make a living ladder. Where their hands pressed they formed the places where new buds and branches would grow. The Twins

led the way up the ladder to the second womb and all the creatures tried to follow. Many fell back however and were later thrown up by Earth in the form of monsters. The second womb was called the Place beneath the Navel. It was broad and high but dark as the earth under storm clouds. The people and the animals increased in number and soon had to struggle to climb the living ladder to a third, and wider world. The Twins sent up the animals and men divided into six groups: yellow, brown-grey, red, white, black and all-colours-mixed. As before, many fell on the way and were later rejected as monsters, cripples and idiots. But in spite of all trials the climb was successful and the fittest creatures survived. At length they entered the world of the Vagina of Earth. The light in this world of sex-birth was like a valley in starlight. Here they discovered the nature of sex and united to bring new life to birth. They developed in many ways. Again they increased in number, and soon, led again by the Preceder and the Follower, animals and men climbed the living ladder of growth into the Womb of Birth, where the light was like the dawn coming in the sky. The Twins began to instruct men, telling them that first of all they should seek the Sun, who would teach them the way of life of the upper world. Each of the tribes understood according to its ability. Their numbers increased until the Twins once again led them onward, this time into the outer world, the World of All-Spreading Light and Seeing.

When men first reached this outer world it was dark. They were strange creatures, black and scaly, with short tails, owls' eyes, huge ears and webbed feet. They were adapted only for the underworld and were hardly able to stand upright. They saw the great star Sirius and thought it must be Sun because its beams hurt their eyes. Then they saw Morning Star still more brilliant, and they mistook that for Sun. But then the sky grew brighter still. The first sunrise was terrible with the howling and terror of the newly emerged human race.

Gradually they grew accustomed to seeing in daylight. When they saw how strange they looked, they made themselves wraps, and sandals to pad their feet against the stony ground.

The new light meant that people discovered many new things. In order to learn all about their wonderful new world, they sought among themselves for people who had been wise even before they came out of their great Earth Mother, the priests. The first of them was Yanauluha. He brought a vessel of water from the great ocean, seeds of plants, and a staff which had power to give life.

The medicine staff of Yanauluha was very beautiful, painted with many colours, and decorated with feathers, shells, and precious minerals. The shells rattled and called the people to see the wonderful staff as it was raised. The priests and people gathered round. Yanauluha lifted the staff, balancing it on one hand while he tapped it sharply with the other. Suddenly four eggs appeared, two white and two blue. The people were told that these were the seeds of living things which would make the summer time more fruitful. They rushed forward to take them. Those who were anxious and eager to get fine things for themselves seized the blue eggs. Those who were not in such haste were content with the white ones. Then the eggs hatched out. The blue eggs produced little coloured birds with rough skins which looked as if they might later be very beautiful. The people fed them well and that made them very greedy by nature. Then feathers grew, shiny black feathers. The newly hatched ravens flew away, laughing raucously at the people who had expected to find beauty in them. Then the plain white eggs hatched and from them flew brilliantly coloured macaws, who were sent off to their home far to the south amid the general rejoicing of the people at seeing such beauty.

After this event the nations were divided into two social groups. The Winter People were those who had chosen Ravens and they were strong and active and many in number. The

Summer People were gentler and slower; their numbers were less but they were the wise and prudent members of the race. From these two the kindred groups were selected at a great council of the people. A few of the totem groups were given the functions of hereditary priests with powers to control the weather and other natural forces. Men were also grouped into sacred societies which would meet to make dances to bring success in the hunt and on the land.

The journeys of man

The emergence of man was completed and the social order established. Men next had to learn how to live in the world under the sun. But the world was new and tormented, with vast swamps inhabited by monsters, desolate plains of broken rock, and earthquakes. It was necessary for men to seek more secure dwelling places. On the journey they were led by the beloved Twins who told them to rest

awhile at a camp called the Place of Uprising which faced the sunrise. At this camp they were instructed to travel towards the east, where Father Sun arose, until they came to the Navel of the Earth. Only there would they find peace and stability.

The people resumed their journey. As yet the world was hardly formed: people were still physically imperfect and fearful in spirit, surrounded by monsters, giants and volcanoes. The Twins held a council and called on Father Sun. In a great hymn they begged for wisdom. The Sun decided that the earth must be broken and turned like a field being dug for planting, and so he and the Twins let fall thunderbolts and lightning. The people cowered in what shelter they could find while the earth was stricken and churned around them. Finally came peace; the monsters had all been destroyed by the thunder and lightning and many perils had disappeared for ever. Sometimes in the

Right. Hemüshikwe kachina mask of painted leather, which represents earth and sky beings. Zuñi, New Mexico. Museum of the American Indian, Heye Foundation, New York.

Far right. Hopi mudhead, or clown, kachina. Arizona. Museum of the American Indian, Heye Foundation, New York.

rocks one can see the bones of the monsters and great areas of broken and scorched rocks which the Zuñi believed resulted from this primeval catastrophe. Then the people rested, protected by the fog-shield of the Twins, before continuing their journey to find the centre, the Navel of the Earth.

Eventually they came to the place where tree-trunks stood in the waters. It was a rich and peaceful land. They thought they had at last reached the Navel of the Earth and built themselves homes. They discovered people who had preceded them, and who were angry and warlike. From them they learned to fight and kill and they became warriors. The day came when the earth shook once more. The leaders sounded the white shell trumpets and the best of the people followed them. Those who were reluctant to leave their homes and property were abandoned and overwhelmed by the destructive force.

The next stage of their journey brought the people to the Place of Mist on the Waters. The mist was the smoke from the fires of a large town. The town-dwellers were peaceful. They told their visitors that they were the elder brothers of men, the People of the Seed. After much discussion a council was held. It was established that it was better to hold to the way of peace than to make war.

After the council they all went to the plains and camped under the cedar and hemlock trees, building a great bower within which sacred symbols were made and prayers chanted. The ceremonies lasted a long time and included dances in which the boys and girls blessed the plants with caresses. Wherever they touched them, the plants burst into coloured flowers with beautiful tendrils. Then the Gods of the Four Seasons appeared from the east, and the food plants prospered. Man was now capable of living freely in the wide world. The events of creation had run their course.

The myth continues with an account of the gradual development of civilisation. Man discovered death; some degenerated and fell back into the lake which led to the lower world. There were further divisions between the people, more struggles with the unstable earth, and continued journeys towards the Navel. Priests were made and ritual societies developed. The gods and kachinas walked with men and in time men lost their tails and became fully human. Those who dwelt at the centre accepted all the movements of the earth and the warnings of the sacred shell trumpets and marched as the gods directed until finally they came to the lands around Zuñi. The myth is long and elaborate and describes many gods and spirits.

Right. Water jar of the Pueblo Indians. The design was intended as a good luck charm, to guide the hunters' arrows to the buffalo's heart. Late 19th century. Museum of Mankind, London.

Below. Karwan and Mana, two kachina figures, who take part in the Powamû ceremony, when the beans which have been artificially sprouted in the kivas are brought out into the plaza and distributed. Smithsonian Institution, Washington, D.C. Bureau of American Ethnology.

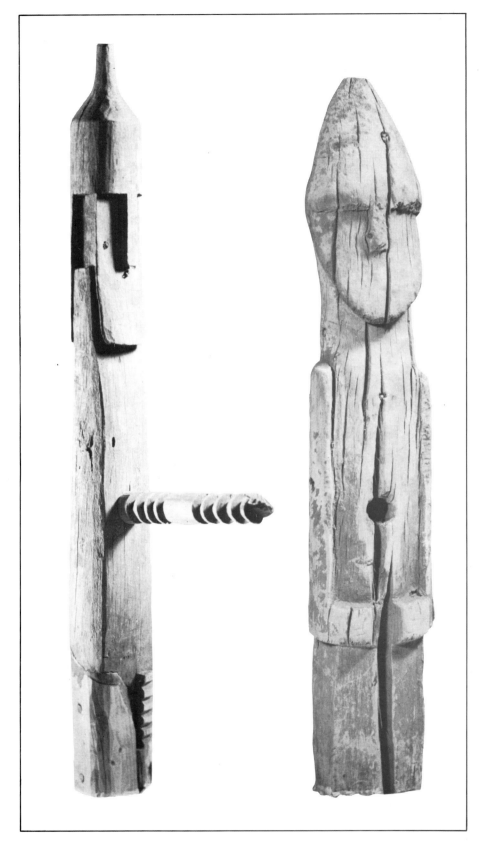

It is all preserved in the chants and ceremonies which were performed until modern times.

The people and the environment

One of the problems presented by the mythology of the Pueblo Indians is the richness and complexity of the material. The relationships between man and natural forces, the animal and the vegetable kingdoms, form the subject of a vast collection of myths which was combined and recombined in long ceremonies in which the myth was re-enacted by costumed actors.

The result was the integration of the people of the pueblo with their natural environment. There was no important event that was not related to man and the gods. Eagles were kept for a year by every family in the pueblo and then killed and sent to the gods to report on the world of men. Man depended on the blessing of the gods; the gods depended on the prayers and magical ceremonies of the people. The social system was naturally disrupted by the impact of the new and wider world of the white man; but there is evidence that the new ways have been assimilated without loss of all the ancient beliefs. A new relationship between man and his environment is evolving and it may be that the influence of North American Indian philosophies and attitudes to life will become more important in the future.

Left. Two war god statuettes of the Zuñi Indians. The Zuñi have two war gods of whom images are made for use in regularly recurring ceremonies. They can only be carved from the wood of pines that have been struck by lightening. The Brooklyn Museum, New York.

Opposite, above. A fetish that formed part of the medicine of one of the Zuñi clans. Chicken feathers, clam shells and turquoises have been attached to a large stone by thongs. Taylor Museum, Colorado Springs Art Center.

Opposite below. 'Shalakos', painted by Philbert Hughie, a Zuni Indian. Indian Pueblo Cultural Center, Albuquerque, New Mexico.

The Past, the Future

The Indian cultures of the North American continent cover a unique range of human activities. They show how the evolution of ideas is intimately linked to the ascending scale of cultural efficiency. At the simplest level, that of the hunter, man's relationship to the spirit world is one of the search for help in obtaining the necessities of daily life. The ancestral spirits as well as the supernatural powers of earth and sky are implored to bring the animals to the hunter. The most powerful spirits seem little different from human beings. But with the advanced groups of agriculturists, it is evident that the more powerful spirits are looked on as gods with well-defined functions and inferior to an almost unknowable First Cause or Great Spirit. The myths describe everyday matters as well as cosmic events and link the whole of creation with man through the emergence myths. Man has to offer prayer and suffering to the gods who are brought into a relationship with the community through rituals which include enactment and recitation of the myths.

Probably the individual's views about the myths in any given tribe also followed an evolutionary sequence. The more backward and the younger individuals would experience the myth in a distinctly more primitive way than the wiser, older chiefs who had a greater knowledge of man and nature in relationship to each other. The shamans were always a special group. Their visions were conditioned by the degree of development of the tribal myths. But in the dissociated condition of the shamanistic trance the type of revelation was fairly consistent. The

Above, left. Making souvenir drums for tourists.

Right. Painting of the Cheyenne Winter Games by Dick West. Philbrook Art Center, Tulsa, Oklahoma.

Opposite. Modern painting of the Buffalo Hunt, a romanticised view of the past, painted by a Navajo artist, Quincy Tahoma. Philbrook Art Center, Tulsa, Oklahoma.

shaman was a prophet rather than a priest. True priesthood hardly existed in the North American Indian cultures. The owners of medicine-bundles had the right to conduct ceremonies, and among the Pueblo Indians the elders who led the activities of the various religious societies had special responsibilities for organisation. But nowhere was there a specialised caste of priests. From the Pueblo Indian stage of development with its leaders of religious societies it is only a small step to a permanent priesthood mediating between man and the spirit world, but it was not fully achieved.

Considered separately, the spirits and gods of North American Indian myths can be classified as archetypal forms arising from the unconscious. The shaman, who dissociates more easily than most people, naturally receives more visions. In the typical shamanistic vision the shaman visits the gods and is able to talk with them. But there is no mention of the shaman being absorbed into the divine personality because his religious understanding is conditioned to the idea of gods who are separate entities from himself. The Indians were able to project their essential beliefs into the form of exterior deities, but did not realise that the archetypal projec-

tions were really part of the individual psyche. Possibly some specially advanced individuals realised that a further stage of religious development might occur when man would be absorbed into the deity, thus making man and his beliefs one whole again, but the myths offer no evidence that this realisation occurred. If the myths truly reflect the condition of the human psyche under primitive conditions of life they constitute a little more evidence for the hope that humanity is evolving towards higher spiritual possibilities as the cultural background develops.

The time scale of human development is almost infinitely variable, but within any given community the development of the mind, the social structure and the economic system are the factors which together give a picture of the whole culture. This book describes the myths that give an important insight into the psychology of a people. It also describes the level of material culture in each group under discussion. Only in this way can we begin to understand the nature of the differences which underlie the ideas common to all men.

The arrival of Europeans had a

devastating effect on Indian society and culture throughout North America. New diseases were introduced which drastically reduced the native population. Increasing dependence on European manufactures destroyed the Indians' self-sufficiency, while the change from a subsistence economy to one based on trading relationships radically altered the structure of tribal society.

But it was the Europeans' territorial ambitions which proved most disruptive to the Indian way of life. With the westward expansion of the United States and Canada, the Indians found their territory and independence increasingly under threat. By the end of the 19th century, the threat had become reality as, through a combination of persuasion, trickery and coercion, the Indians were dispossessed of their traditional hunting grounds. Treaties promising farms, equipment, annuities and services in return for land cessions proved worthless or ineffectual, and attempts to resist territorial encroachment or the violation of treaty rights were put down with military force.

Confined to small and isolated reservations, often with limited econ-omic potential, and administered by a cumbersome and restrictive bureaucracy, the Indians became increasingly demoralised, their confidence and self-respect destroyed by the imposition of an alien social structure. Their traditional hunting existence was actively discouraged. Their cultural and spiritual values were disparaged and ceremonies like the Sun Dance and potlatch were outlawed. Their children were removed to boarding schools, where, forbidden to speak their own language, they were instructed in the manners, attitudes and accomplishments of their white conquerers.

To be fair, such measures were often well-intentioned, many whites genuinely believing that assimilation into the mainstream society would be most beneficial for the Indian. In the end, however, they proved catastrophic, undermining family ties, group identity and cultural integrity and, together with intense material deprivation, leading to the social and psychological breakdown of whole communities.

The Inuit were also subjected to similar misguided and destructive policies and have suffered the same social ills resulting from them. However, they have probably been affected less than other groups, since their land did not attract the same degree of colonial development and they managed to remain in the majority.

Today, in spite of more enlightened attitudes and policies, particularly over the past two decades, and in spite of the growing articulacy and militancy of their own leaders, the

native peoples still remain the most disadvantaged section in North American society, suffering from chronic unemployment, bad housing and disease, with a high incidence of delinquency, vagrancy, alcoholism and suicide, and their demands for educational reform, new approaches to land and treaty rights and, above all, the right to self-determination, have yet to be realised.

When these myths were recorded most of the North American Indian tribes were already dispersed. Only among the Inuit, the Pueblo and the Navajo peoples did the mythology represent a living religious cult. A few centuries of change had largely altered the religious observances of the other tribes into either social observances or folklore. In particular the traditions of the Indians of the southeastern states had become the heritage of only a few old people.

Since then the process has continued much further and many Indians have found that traditions have only been preserved through the work of white ethnologists at the turn

of the century, who recorded what then survived. This does not mean that myths have totally lost their power, but they have tended to assume the nature of folk tales. Here and there one may find a true shaman with gifts of prophecy and healing, who has preserved some traditions, but such people are few. Some of the tales told to Indian children preserve a little of the past, and many of the customs intended to bring good luck, and avert bad, have remained.

Some tribes have retained echoes of their ancient tribal organisation and still reverence the ancestral traditions. The Iroquois people, particularly, remember the ancient ceremonial and place it successfully in a modern setting. The Pueblos still sing some of the ancient chants and the religious dances are publicly performed, though often largely for the benefit of tourists. Thus the impact of the new culture has not totally destroyed the past. Indeed there are signs that the tide is turning, with a growing political and cultural awareness among Indians of all groups. There is

a revival of interest and pride in the old ways. Old crafts are being revived, old stories and songs relearned. While adjustment to western ways and values has put a strain on the social, economic and intellectual life of the Indians, at the same time, increasing involvement in white society has given many the experience and confidence to stand up for their rights and beliefs. The growing pan-Indian movement, often called Red Power, seeks to regain for the Indians their ethnic identity and the control over their own lives lost during the last 200 years.

Now that the Indian heritage is coming to be highly regarded in North America, the philosophy behind the myths has been sought after and preserved. A notable piece of preservation has been the collection of Navajo sand-paintings which are changed at the appropriate seasons in the Museum of Navajo Ceremonial Art in Santa Fe. This allows visitors to appreciate that sand-paintings illustrate the relationship between man and nature, and the

The Inuit have a new way of life, and new possibilities of graphic expression. The modern soapstone carvings and the lithographs have great elegance and good rhythmic form and spatial relationships, but few of them reflect the folk tales which survive from the old myths of man and the spirit world. When they do they are made for an alien viewer and, like so much magic, become aesthetic expressions without any genuine contact with myth.

Perhaps the best way to appreciate the ancient myths of the world is to regard them as an expression of the deepest beliefs of the people who made them. They have faded with time simply because the ways of human life have changed. Yet every nation has its heritage of tradition and that tradition has influenced the quality of intellectual life in its present-day representatives. One hopes that the North American Indian myths will prove to be acceptable and enlightening to the modern world.

Above. A modern totem pole emerges on Canada's west coast.

Left. An Indian encampment at Banff, Alberta. For special occasions the Indians sometimes recreate a life-style that is gone. The Royal Canadian Mounted Police, who contributed much to the comparatively peaceful settlement of Canada's West, and who early on won the respect of the Indians, are still the premier police force in the country.

Opposite. Modern acrylic painting 'Wee-Sa-Kay-Jac and the Magic Mishipizhiw' by Samuel Ash, Ojibwa, Lake St. Joseph Reserve, Ontario, Canada.

passage of the stars in the heavens. In such ways the myths are becoming part of the cultural heritage of North America, and ultimately of all men.

The Indian myths have affected modern art to some extent, but more through their technique than their philosophy. Similarly with the very active tradition of the Pueblo potters and weavers. The beauty of the craftsmanship is universally accepted but the meaning of the designs very rarely matters even to the craftsmen themselves.

Chief Gods and Spirits of North America

Inuit

AKYCHA: Alaskan name of the Sun.

ANINGAN: the Moon.

ARNARQUAGSSAQ: Greenland name of Sedna.

IDLIRVIRISSONG: demonic cousin of the Sun.

IGALUK: Alaskan name of the Moon.

NANOOK (NANUQ): the Bear. The Pleiades.

NEGAFOK: the cold weather spirit.

NERIVIK: Alaskan name of Sedna.

SEDNA: Central Inuit name of the great Sea Mother.

SEQINEK: the Sun.

SIUDLERATUIN: the spirits of the dead.

TORNAQ: a spirit being, the familiar of a shaman.

TORNARSUK (THE SEPARATE TORNAQ): a superior spirit.

Northwest Coast

ADEE (OR IDI): the Thunderbird.

DZARILAW: the Bear Prince, a protean animal hero.

DZELARHONS: Haida name of a Volcano Woman and a Frog Princess.

GUNARH: the mythical Killer Whale.

GUNARHNESENGYET: Tlingit hero, a great hunter.

GYHLDEPTIS (HANGING-HAIR): a vegetation spirit.

MEITLIKH: Lightning Snake.

KANNUCK: the Wolf Spirit.

KEAGYIHL DEPGUESK: the Spirit of the Whirlpool.

QAGWAAI: a hero, destroyer of monsters. Also the name sometimes given to the monster itself.

NEEGYAUKS: Tlingit name of Dzelarhons.

RHPISUNT: Haida name of Bear Mother.

SKYAMSEN: Tlingit name of the Thunderbird.

TLENAMAW: a monstrous dragon.

TSECTS: grandmother white mouse, a friendly spirit.

YEHL: the Raven, a demiurge and a Trickster.

Northern Forests

BETSUNE YENECA: Ojibwa name of the Old Woman's Grandchild, a magic boy from the stars.

DJENETA: Ojibwa name of a giant.

GLUSKAP: the creator force in Algonkian myth.

HALBOREDJA: Means 'day wanderer'. The Sun.

HERECGUNINA: The power of evil.

HEROK'A: 'Those without horns' — Earth Spirits.

HOCEREU WAHIRA: The Disease-Bringer.

MALSUM: the destructive force in Algonkian myth. Brother to Gluskap.

MAUNA: The Earth-Maker.

MIDEWEWIN: Ojibwa name of a society of shamans.

NANABOJO or WINABOJO: Ojibwa name of the Trickster, the Master of Life.

OCKABEWIS: Ojibwa name of the messenger of the gods, and teacher of mankind.

WAKTCEXI: A water-monster.

WAXCPINI XEDERA: The Great Spirit.

WISAGATCAK: the Cree name of the Trickster.

Eastern Woodlands

DEOHAKO: Iroquois spirits of corn, beans and squash.

GAOH: Iroquois name of the Master of the Winds.

GITCHE MANITOU: the All-Father, great spirit.

HAIO HWA THA: Mohawk chief and Great Lawgiver, known to the white man as Hiawatha.

MA NEGOATEGEH: Iroquois name of the evil Twin.

HA WEN NEYU: Iroquois name of the Great Spirit.

HAMEDICU: Huron name of the High God.

HENG (OR DE HI NO): Huron name of Thunder.

HENO (OR HINU): Iroquois name of Thunder and a male fertility spirit.

HONOCHENOKEH: Iroquois name of the Invisible Helpers, spirits of goodwill.

HUTI WATSI YA: Huron name of the Pleiades.

KETQ SKWAYE: Huron Creator. Grandmother Toad.

ORENDA: Iroquois supernatural force.

TARHUHYIAWAHKU: Iroquois name of a Giant, the holder of the heavens.

TAWESKARE (OR TAWISKARO): Huron name of the evil Creator-Twin.

TSENTSA: Huron name of the good Creator-Twin.

The Great Plains

ANGPETU WI: Dakota name meaning the Sun.

ANPAO: Dakota name of the Dawn.

ANUNGITE: Dakota name meaning two-faced being.

AWAHOKSHU: Pawnee Abode of Spiritual Power.

CHAHURU: Pawnee name of the Water Spirit.

CHIXU: Pawnee name of the Ghosts.

CIRAPE: Crow name of the Little Coyote, younger brother of the Trickster.

HANGHEPI WI: Dakota name of the Moon and Night.

HENGA: Osage name of the Sacred Eagle.

HEYOKA: Dakota name of a group of deities, The Opposites.

HOITA: Mandan Spotted Eagle spirit.

HOKEWINGLA: Dakota name of the Turtle-man in the Moon.

HONGA: Osage name of the Earth People, living below ground.

HOTORU: Pawnee name of the wind god.

H'URARU: Pawnee name of the Earth Spirit.

ISAKAKATE: Crow name of the Supreme being.

ISAKAWUATE: Crow name of Old Man Coyote, the Trickster.

KECKAMANETOWA: Fox name of the gentle manitou.

KETCHIMANETOWA: Fox name of the Great Spirit.

MAHO PENETA: Mandan name of the Great Spirit.

MAHO PENEKHEKA: Mandan name of the Evil power.

MAH SISH: Mandan name of the War Eagle.

MAMA'SA'A: Fox name of the First Man.

MANINGA: Mandan flood spirit.

MEDI KENAGA: Fox name of the Great Snapping Turtle.

MENAHKA: Mandan name of the Sun.

MIKAK'E: Osage name of the Star People.

NESARU: the Arikara name for The Power Above.

NUMOKH MUKANA: Mandan name of the First Man.

OKE HEDE: Mandan name of the Evil Twin.

SHAKURU: Pawnee name of the Sun.

TAKUSKANSKAN: Dakota name of the Moving God, the wind, and a Trickster.

TIRAWA ATIUS: Pawnee name of the Great Power.

TSI-ZHUI: Osage name of the Sky People.

TTLAYA: Fox name of a ghost.

TUNKAN INGAN: Dakota name of a sex god.

UNKTEHI: Dakota name of a water spirit.

UTI HIATA: Pawnee name of Mother Corn.

WAKINYAN: Dakota name of Thunder.

WAKONDA: Osage and Dakota name of the Power Above.

WALA: Fox name of the Dawn.

WASICONG: Dakota name of a protective spirit.

The Southwest

DELGETH: the flesh-eating antelope.

ESTANATLEHI: Woman who recreates herself: the most respected Navajo deity, helper of mankind.

GLISPA: culture heroine of the Navajo.

HASTSEHOGAN: God of the House.

HASTSELTSI: Red Lord, god of racing.

HASTSEOLTOI: goddess of hunting, wife of war god.

HASTSEYALTI or YEBITSAI: Maternal Grandfather of the Gods, the Talking God, creator.

HASTSEZINI: Black Lord, the fire god.

NAGENATZANI: Elder Twin Brother, son of Estanatlehi.

THOBADESTCHIN: Younger Twin Brother, son of Estanatlehi.

TIEHOLTSODI: the Navajo water monster.

TLEHANOAI: Carrier of Night, the moon god.

TOBADZISTSINI: Child of the Waterfall, a war spirit.

TO'NENILE: rain god.

TSOTSIL: magical boundary mountain of the Navajo.

YEBAAD: Female leader of the gods.

YEBA KA: Male leader of the gods.

YEITSO: the Sun's child. A giant in Navajo legend.

The Southeast

ANITSUTSA: Cherokee name of the Pleiades.

AWAHILI: Cherokee name of a sacred eagle.

GEYAGUGA: Magical Cherokee name of the Moon.

HELOHA: Choctaw name of the female Thunderbird.

HISAKITAIMISI: Creek name of the Controller of Life.

HITCHI: Hitchiti name of the first tobacco plant.

INAGI-UTASUNHI: Cherokee name of the Dark Twin, a wild boy.

ISTEPAHPAH: Creek name of a devouring monster.

KANATI (male) and SELU (female): Cherokee name of the First Ancestors.

KOTI: Creek name of a water-frog, a helpful spirit.

LUDJATAKO: Creek name of the Giant Turtle.

MELATHA: Choctaw name of the male Lightningbird.

MICUX: Natchez name of a heroine, the human daughter of a cannibal spirit.

NANIH WAIYA: Choctaw name meaning 'Bending Hill' – the place of emergence; later used as a name for the Creator.

NUNYUNUWI: Cherokee name meaning 'Dressed in Stone' – a destructive cannibal spirit.

OHOYO OSH CHISHBA: Choctaw name meaning 'Unknown Woman' – a name of the Corn Mother.

OKLATABASHIH: Choctaw name meaning 'The Mourner of the People' – the survivor from the Flood.

PASIKOLA: Creek name of the Rabbit, the Trickster.

SHAKANLI: Choctaw name of the animal monster.

SHILUP: Choctaw name of a ghost.

SHILUP CHITO OSH: Choctaw name of the Great Spirit.

SUTALIDIHI: Cherokee name of Unelanunhi, the Sun.

TLANUWA: Cherokee name of the Great Hawk, a magic bird. Natchez name of a magical bird with metal feathers.

TSALU: Cherokee name of tobacco.

UKTENA: Cherokee name of the Great Water Serpent.

UKTENI: Natchez name of a magical water snake.

UNELANUNHI: Cherokee name of the Sun.

UTSANATI: Cherokee Rattlesnake, helper of man.

Pueblo

AMITOLANE: Zuñi name of the Rainbow.

AWONAWILONA: the First Cause in Pueblo myth.

HAHAI WÜGTI: Hopi name of the Spider Woman.

IATIKU AND NAUTSITI: Acoma name of the Sisters who created man.

KASTIATSI: Acoma name of the Rainbow.

KATSINAS: Acoma name of the younger children of Iatiku, with powers to bring rain and food.

KERWAN and KATCINA MANA: Hopi name of the Sprouting Maize Spirits.

KOSHARI: Sia name of the First Man.

MASEWI and OYOYEWI: Acoma name of the Twins, War Spirits.

MAYOCHINA: Acoma name of the Summer Spirit.

MOMO: Hopi name of the Honeybee.

MORITYAMA: Acoma name of the Spring Spirit.

PAUTIWA: Hopi name of the Sun.

PALULUKON: Hopi name of the Great Serpent.

PISHUMI: Acoma name of the Spirit of Disease.

POSHAIYANGKYO: Zuñi Father of all Medicine and the First Man.

QUERRANA: Sia name of the Second Man.

SHAKAK: Acoma name of the Winter Spirit.

SHRUISTHIA: Acoma name of the Autumn Spirit.

SIO CALAKO: Hopi name of a Giant.

SIO HUMIS: Hopi name of a Rain Spirit.

SKOYO: Sia name of the devouring monsters.

SOYOKO: Generic Hopi name for monsters.

SUSSISTINNAKO: Sia name of the Spider in Darkness – the First Being.

TCOLAWITZE: Hopi name of Fire.

TEHABI: Hopi name of Mudhead, the clown.

TIAMUNI: Acoma name of the First Man.

TSICHTINAKA: Acoma name of the guide of mankind during the emergence.

UCHTSITI: Acoma name meaning 'nothing lacking' – Father of the Gods.

UTSET and BOWUTSET: Sia name of the First Mothers.

WILOLANE: Zuñi name of the Lightning.

YANAULUHA: Zuñi name given to the First Priest.

Further Reading List

Carpenter, E., *Eskimo Realities*. Holt, Rinehart & Winston, New York, 1973.

Catlin, George, *The Manners, Customs and Condition of the North American Indians*. G. Catlin, London, 1841. (Reprinted in new edition by Dover Publications, New York, 1973).

Clark, E. E., *Indian Legends of the Pacific Northwest*. Cambridge University Press, 1958.

Collier, John, *Indians of the Americas – The Long Hope*. W. W. Norton & Co., New York, 1947.

Deloria, Vine, Jr., *God is Red*. Dell Publications Co. Inc., New York, 1973.

Driver Harold, *Indians of North America*. University of Chicago Press, 1967.

Judson, K. B., *Myths and Legends of Alaska*. University of Chicago Press, 1911.

La Farge, Oliver, *A Pictorial History of the American Indians*. Spring Books, London, 1862.

MacCulloch, John A., and Gray, Louis H., *North American Mythology* in *The Mythology of All Races*. 13 vols. Cooper Square Pubs. Inc., New York, 1922.

Macmillan, C., *Glooscap's Country*. Oxford University Press, 1956.

Nungak, Z. and Arima, E., *Eskimo Stories/Unikkaatuat*. Ottawa, 1969.

Palmer, Wm. Rees, *Why the North Star Stands Still*. Bailey Bros. & Swinfen, London, 1957.

Snow, Dean, *The Archaeology of North America. American Indians and their Origins*, Thames & Hudson, inc. New York, 1980.

Spence, Lewis, *Myths and Legends of the North American Indians*. Harrap, London, 1914.

Turner, G., *Indians of North America*. Blandford Press, Poole, Dorset, 1979.

Underhill, Ruth, *Red Man's Religion. Beliefs and Practices of the Indians North of Mexico*. University of Chicago Press, 1966.

Wood, Marion, Spirits, *Heroes and Hunters from North American Indian Mythology*. Peter Lowe 1981.

Acknowledgments

American Museum of National History, New York 32 right, 104; Ashmolean Museum, Oxford 113 left; B.B.C. Hulton Picture Library, London 41 bottom; David Barber, AV/TV Services, University of Regina 138 top; Bildarchiv Foto Marburg 55 right, 93 bottom left; British Museum, London 20 top, 23, 24–5 bottom, 36, 41 top, 44, 58–9, 68 left, 97, 117 left; Brooklyn Museum, New York 105, 132 left, 132 right; Camera Press, London 95, 127; Canadian High Commission, London 11 left, 11 right, 22 top left, 47 bottom, 52–3, 139 top, 139 bottom; Cincinnati Art Museum, Ohio 112 left; Michael Dent 26–7, 62–3, 123; Denver Art Museum, Colorado 34, 83; Exeter University, American Arts Department 8, 9, 17; Field Museum of Natural History, Chicago, Illinois 46; Werner Forman Archive, London 39; Founders Society, Detroit Institute of Arts, Michigan 58; Glenbow-Alberta Institute, Calgary 37 top; Hamlyn Publishing, Twickenham 33, 138 bottom; Michael Holford, Loughton 103; Horniman Museum, London 10–11, 99; Kansas State Historical Society, Topeka 10 right; Larousse 77; Linden-Museum, Stuttgart 88–9; Metropolitan Museum of Art, New York 76 top right, 109 bottom, 122 left; Museum of the American Indian, Heye Foundation, New York half-title page, 10 left, 20 bottom, 21 left, 32 left, 45 top, 45 bottom, 50, 51, 55 left, 56, 56–7, 63, 67, 69, 70 left, 79, 80, 87, 89 top, 89 bottom, 93 top left, 109 top, 111, 117 right, 118, 119, 125, 130 left, 130 right; Museum of Modern Art New York 14 top; Museum of Navajo Ceremonial Art, Santa Fé, New Mexico 94, 100–1; National Archives, Washington, D.C.–U.S. Signal Corps 14 bottom, 14–15; Nationalmuseet, Copenhagen 25, 68 bottom right; Newnes Books, Feltham 13, 21 right, 22 top right, 22 bottom, 24–25 top, 38 top, 42, 43, 48–9, 65, 70 centre, 82, 110, 112 top right, 114 left, 114 top right, 114 bottom right, 116, 121, 122 right, 124, 126 left, 129, 131 top, 131 bottom; New York State Museum and Science Service, Albany 61, 70 right; Ohio State Development Department 108; Pacific Northern Airlines, Inc. 29; Peabody Museum of Archaeology and Ethnology, Harvard University, Cambridge, Massachusetts 113 right; Philbrook Art Center, Tulsa, Oklahoma 136–7 top, 136–7 bottom, 137; Photoresources, Canterbury 47 top; The Photo Source/Colour Library International, London 18–19, 74, 74–5, 102, 106–7, 133 bottom, 134–5; Rijksmuseum voor Volkenkunde, Leiden 54 right, 93 right; Rochester Museum of Arts and Sciences, Rochester, New York 68 top right, 71; Royal Scottish Museum, Edinburgh frontispiece; Smithsonian Institution, Washington, D.C., Bureau of American Ethnology 12, 15, 31, 38 bottom, 40, 73, 76 top left, 76 bottom left, 81, 84–5, 86, 122 right, 131 bottom; Smithsonian Institution, Washington, D.C., Museum of Natural History 78; Smithsonian Institution, United States National Museum 76 bottom right; Staatliches Museum für Völkerkunde, Dresden 37 bottom; Staatliches Museum für Völkerkunde, Munich 54 left; Taylor Museum, Colorado Springs 28, 35, 126 right, 133 top; University Museum, Philadelphia, Pennsylvania 18, 30; Marion Wood 90–1.

Index